Computing
Made Simple

CW00727582

Access 2000
STEPHEN
0750641827   1999

Access 2000 Business Edition
STEPHEN
075064611X   1999

Access 97 for Windows
STEPHEN
0750638001   1997

CompuServe 2000   `NEW!`
BRINDLEY
0750645245   2000

Designing Internet Home Pages
2nd edition
HODBS
0750644761   1999

ECDL/ICDL Version 3.0   `NEW!`
BCD
0750651873   2000

Excel 2000
MORRIS
0750641800   2000

Excel 2000 Business Edition
MORRIS
0750646098   2000

Excel 97 for Windows
MORRIS
0750638028   1997

Excel for Windows 95 (V. 7)
MORRIS
0750628162   1996

Explorer 5
MCBRIDE, P K
0750646276   1999

Frontpage 2000
MCBRIDE, Nat
0750645989   1999

FrontPage 97
MCBRIDE, Nat
0750639415   1998

iMac and iBook   `NEW!`
BRINDLEY
075064608X   2000

Internet In Colour
2nd edition
MCBRIDE, P K
0750645768   1999

Internet for Windows 98
MCBRIDE, P K
0750645636   1999

MS DOS
SINCLAIR
0750620692   1994

Office 2000
MCBRIDE, P K
0750641797   1999

Office 97
MCBRIDE, P K
0750637986   1997

Outlook 2000   `NEW!`
MCBRIDE, P K
0750644141   2000

Photoshop
WYNNE-POWELL
075064334X   1999

Pocket PC   `NEW!`
PEACOCK
0750649003   2000

Powerpoint 2000
STEPHEN
0750641770   1999

Powerpoint 97 for Windows
STEPHEN
0750637994   1997

Publisher 2000
STEPHEN
0750645970   1999

Publisher 97
STEPHEN
0750639431   1998

Sage Accounts
McBRIDE
0750644133   1999

Searching the Internet
MCBRIDE, P K
0750637943   1998

Windows 98   `NEW!`
MCBRIDE, P K
0750640391   1998

Windows 95
MCBRIDE, P K
0750623063   1995

Windows CE
PEACOCK
0750643358   1999

Windows ME   `NEW!`
MCBRIDE, P K
0750652373   2000

Windows NT
HOBBS
0750635118   1997

Word 2000
BRINDLEY
0750641819   1999

Word 2000 Business Edition
BRINDLEY
0750646101   2000

Word 97 for Windows
BRINDLEY
075063801X   1997

Word 7 for Windows 95
BRINDLEY
0750628154   1996

Works 2000
MCBRIDE, P K
0750649852   2000

UPCOMING in 2001

Basic Computer Skills
SHERMAN
075064897X

ECDL/ICDL 3.0
Office 2000 Edition
BCD
0750653388

Microsoft Project 2000
MURPHY
0750651903

ALL YOU NEED TO GET STARTED!

MADE SIMPLE BOOKS

Programming Made Simple

C Programming
SEXTON
0750632445   1997

C++ Programming
SEXTON
0750632437   1997

COBOL
SEXTON
0750638346   1998

Delphi Version 5   NEW!
MORRIS
0750651881   2000

Delphi
MORRIS
0750632461   1997

HTML 4.0
MCBRIDE
0750641789   1999

Java
MCBRIDE, P K
0750632410   1997

Javascript
MCBRIDE, P K
0750637978   1997

Pascal
MCBRIDE, P K
0750632429   1997

Visual Basic
MORRIS
0750632453   1997

Visual C++
MORRIS
0750635703   1998

ALL YOU NEED TO GET STARTED!

MADE SIMPLE
BOOKS

Windows® XP
Made Simple

P.K. McBride

MADE SIMPLE
BOOKS

OXFORD · AMSTERDAM · BOSTON · HEIDELBERG · LONDON · NEW YORK · PARIS
SAN DIEGO · SAN FRANCISCO · SINGAPORE · SYDNEY · TOKYO

Made Simple
An imprint of Elsevier Science
Linacre House, Jordan Hill, Oxford 0X2 8DP
200 Wheeler Road, Burlington, MA 01803

First published 2002
Reprinted 2003 (twice)

TRADEMARKS/REGISTERED TRADEMARKS
Computer hardware and software brand names mentioned in this book are
protected by their respective trademarks and are acknowledged

British Library Cataloguing in Publication Data
A catalogue record for this book is available from the British Library

Library of Congress Cataloging in Publication Data
A catalogue record for this book is available from the Library of Congress

ISBN 0 7506 5626 3

For information on all Made Simple publications
visit our website at www.madesimple.co.uk

Typeset by McBride

Printed and bound in Great Britain by Scotprint

Contents

Preface IX

1 Start here   1

The Desktop 2
Taming the mouse 4
The keyboard 5
Making choices 6
Context menus 8
The Start menu 9
Running a program 10
Logging off and on 11
Shutting down 12
Coping with crashes 13
Summary 14

2 Help!   15

Help with applications 16
Finding Help 20
Help and Support 22
Instant Help 26
Summary 28

3 Window control   29

The window frame 30
Window modes 32
Arranging windows 34
Moving windows 36
Changing the size 37
Scrolling 38
Closing windows 39
Summary 40

4	Exploring folders	41
	The four faces of Explorer	42
	Files and folders	43
	Windows Explorer	46
	My Computer	47
	Customizing the toolbar	51
	Folder Options	52
	Expanding folders	54
	Creating a folder	56
	Moving folders	58
	Deleting folders	59
	Summary	60

5	Managing files	61
	Arranging files	62
	Selecting sets of files	64
	Moving and copying	66
	Deleting files	68
	The Recycle Bin	69
	Finding files	70
	Properties	72
	Shortcuts	74
	File Types	77
	Summary	78

6	The Taskbar	79
	Taskbar options	80
	Taskbar toolbars	82
	The Start menu	84
	Organising the menu	86
	Setting the Clock	87
	Summary	88

7	The Control Panel	89
	The settings	90
	Appearance and Themes	92
	Adjusting the mouse	97
	Sounds	99
	Regional options	100
	Accessibility	102
	Fonts	104
	Summary	106
8	Printers	107
	Printer settings	108
	Adding a printer	110
	Managing the queue	112
	Direct printing	113
	Summary	114
9	Disk housekeeping	115
	The System Tools	116
	Error-checking	118
	Disk Defragmenter	119
	Backup	120
	Disk Cleanup	123
	Add/Remove Programs	124
	System Restore	126
	Formatting a floppy	128
	Caring for floppies	129
	Summary	130
10	Users and networks	131
	User Accounts	132
	Changing user details	134

Networking 136

Network Setup Wizard 138

Sharing access 140

Mapped drives 142

Summary 144

11 The Accessories 145

WordPad 146

NotePad 150

The Character Map 151

Paint 152

Picture and Fax Viewer 156

Scanner/Camera Wizard 158

Media Player 159

Movie Maker 161

Summary 162

12 Exploring the Internet 163

Internet Explorer 164

Starting to explore 166

The History list 167

Favorites 168

Searching in Explorer 170

Windows Update 172

Radio stations 174

Outlook Express 176

Summary 178

Index 179

Preface

Windows, in its various forms, is now established as the world's leading operating system for personal computers. Windows XP is the latest version, and the first to be designed for both home and office users.

Windows XP Made Simple has been written mainly for the new computer user. It aims to give you enough to be able to start using Windows quickly and confidently. Once you have got into the Windows' way of doing things, you will find it easy to extend your skills and knowledge.

In the first three chapters you will learn about the basic concepts and techniques of working with Windows – making choices, using the Help system and managing the screen.

Chapters 4 and 5 will show you how to organise your disks, so that you can store files safely and efficiently – and find them when you want them. We return to disks in Chapter 9, where we'll look at how to keep them in good working order.

One of the attractive features of Windows is that it lets you customise your system to suit the way that you work. In Chapters 6 and 7 you will see how to do this. Another of its attractive features is the ease with which it can be connected to peripherals and other PCs. You will see this in Chapters 8 and 10, *Printers* and *Users and networks*.

In Chapter 11, we will have a quick look at a few of the accessories, then in the final chapter we will step away from the desktop into the wider world of the Internet. There is no space in this small book to do justice to this vast topic, but I hope that you will at least get a sense of its possibilities – then turn to *The Internet Made Simple* to find out more!

P.K. McBride, 2002

Take note

PCs running earlier version of Windows can be upgraded to Windows XP providing that they have sufficient RAM (minimum 64Mb, but realistically 128Mb). Before you do upgrade, go to Microsoft's site and check that your existing peripherals and software will work with XP – there are many known compatibility problems.

1 Start here

The Desktop 2

Taming the mouse 4

The keyboard 5

Making choices 6

Context menus 8

The Start menu 9

Running a program 10

Logging off and on 11

Shutting down 12

Coping with crashes 13

Summary 14

The Desktop

Windows is a Graphical User Interface (or GUI, pronounced *gooey*). What this means is that you work mainly by using the mouse to point at and click on symbols on the screen, rather than by typing commands. It is largely intuitive – i.e. the obvious thing to do is probably the right thing – and it is tolerant of mistakes. Many can be corrected as long as you tackle them straight away, and many others can be corrected easily, even after time has passed.

One of the key ideas behind the design of Windows is that you should treat the screen as you would a desk, which is why Windows refers to the screen as the *desktop*. This is where you lay out your papers, books and tools, and you can arrange them to suit your own way of working. You may want to have more than one set of papers on the desktop at a time – so Windows lets you run several programs at once. You may want to have all your papers visible, for comparing or transferring data; you may want to concentrate on one, but have the others to hand. These – and other arrangements – are all possible.

Each program runs in its own window, and these can be arranged side by side, overlapping, or with the one you are working on filling the desktop and the others tucked out of the way, but still instantly accessible.

Just as there are many ways of arranging your desktop, so there are many ways of working with it – in fact, you are sometimes spoilt for choice!

It's your desktop. How you arrange it, and how you use it is up to you. This book will show you the simplest ways to use Windows XP effectively.

❑ What you see on screen when you start Windows depends upon your Desktop settings and the shortcuts – the icons that you can click on to start progams – you are using.

❑ What the screen looks like once you are into your working session, is infinitely variable.

❑ Certain principles always apply and certain things are always there. It is the fact that all Windows applications share a common approach that makes Windows so easy to use.

Shortcuts – instant access to programs. You can create shortcuts (page 74).

Desktop – you can change the background picture or pattern and its colours (page 94).

Menu bar – gives access to a program's commands.

Program windows – adjust their size and placing to suit yourself.

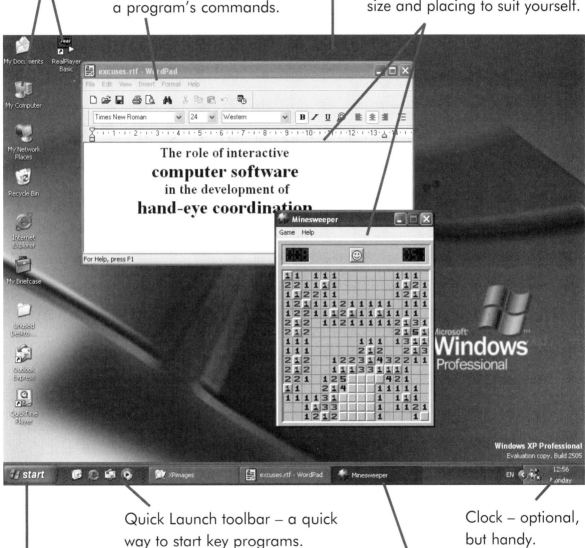

Quick Launch toolbar – a quick way to start key programs.

Clock – optional, but handy.

Start button – you should be able to start any program on your PC from its menu.

Taskbar – when a program is running, it has a button here. Click on a button to open its window and bring it to the front of the desktop.

Taming the mouse

You can't do much in Windows until you have tamed the mouse. It is used for locating the cursor, for selecting from menus, highlighting, moving and changing the size of objects, and much more. It won't bite, but it will wriggle until you have shown it who's in charge.

To control the mouse effectively you need a mouse mat or a thin pad of paper – mice don't run well on hard surfaces.

The mouse and the cursor

Moving the mouse rolls the ball inside it. The ball turns the sensor rollers and these transmit the movement to the cursor. Straightforward? Yes, but note these points.

● If you are so close to the edge of the mat that you cannot move the cursor any further, pick up the mouse and plonk it back into the middle. If the ball doesn't move, the cursor doesn't move.

● You can set up the mouse so that when the mouse is moved faster, the cursor moves further (see *Adjusting the mouse*, page 97). Watch out for this when working on other people's machines.

Tip

A clean mouse is a happy mouse. If it starts to play up, take out the ball and clean it and the rollers with a damp tissue. Check for fluff build-up on the roller axles and remove any present with tweezers.

Mouse actions

Point – move the cursor with your fingers off the buttons.

Click the left button to select a file, menu item or other object.

Right-click (click the right button) to open a menu of commands that can be applied to the object beneath the pointer.

Double-click to run programs. You can set the gap between clicks to suit yourself (see *Adjusting the mouse*, page 97).

Drag – keep the left button down while moving the mouse. Used for resizing, drawing and similar jobs.

Drag and drop – drag an object and release the left button when it is in the right place. Used for moving objects.

Key guide

[Esc] – to Escape from trouble. Use it to cancel bad choices.

[Tab] – move between objects on screen.

[Caps Lock] – only put this on when you want to type a lot of capitals. The Caps Lock light shows if it is on.

[Shift] – use it for capitals and the symbols on the number keys.

[Ctrl] or [Control] – used with other keys to give keystroke alternatives to mouse commands.

▨ – same as clicking ⊞ start on the screen.

[Alt] – used, like [Ctrl], with other keys.

[Backspace] – rubs out the character to the left of the text cursor.

[Enter] – used at the end of a piece of text or to start an operation.

[Delete] – deletes files, folders and screen objects. Use with care.

The keyboard

Most Windows XP operations can be handled quite happily by the mouse alone, leaving the keyboard for data entry. However, keys are necessary for some jobs, and if you prefer typing to mousing, it is possible to do most jobs from the keyboard. The relevant ones are shown here.

The function keys

Some operations can be run from these – for instance, **[F1]** starts up the Help system in any Windows application.

The control sets

The **Arrow** keys can often be used instead of the mouse for moving the cursor. Above them are more movement keys, which will let you jump around in text. **[Insert]** and **[Delete]** are also here.

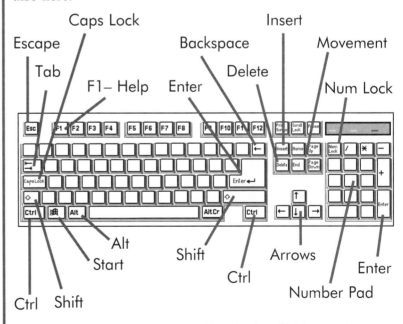

Num Lock ON for numbers
OFF for movement

5

Making choices

There are many situations where you have to specify a filename or an option. Sometimes you have to type in what you want, but in most cases, it only takes a click of the mouse or a couple of keystrokes.

Menus

To pull one down from the menu bar click on it, or press **[Alt]** (the key marked '**Alt**') and the underlined letter – usually the initial.

To select an item from a menu, click on it or type its underlined letter.

Some items are *toggles*. Selecting them turns an option on or off. ✔ beside the name shows that the option is on.

▶ after an item shows that another menu leads from it.

If you select an item with three dots ... after it, a dialog box will open to get more information from you.

Dialog boxes

These vary, but will usually have:

- ⬤ ⬓OK⬓ to click when you have set the options, selected the file or whatever;

- ⬤ ⬓Apply⬓ fix the options selected so far, but do not leave the box;

- ⬤ ⬓Cancel⬓ in case you decide the whole thing was a mistake;

- ⬤ ⬓?⬓ to get Help on items in the box.

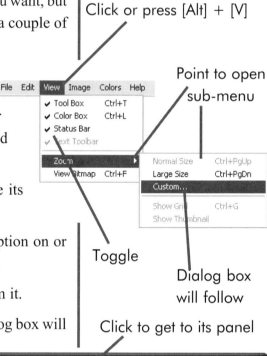

Click or press [Alt] + [V]

Point to open sub-menu

Toggle

Dialog box will follow

Click to get to its panel

Tabs and panels

Some dialog boxes have several sets of options in them, each on a separate panel. These are identified by tabs at the top. Click on a tab to bring its panel to the front. Usually clicking [OK] on any panel will close the whole box. Use [Apply] when you have finished with one panel but want to explore others before closing.

Check boxes

These are used where there are several options, and you can use as many as you like at the same time.

✔ in the box shows that the option has been selected.

If the box is grey and the caption faint, the option is 'greyed out' – not available at that time for the selected item.

Radio buttons

These are used for either/or options. Only one of the set can be selected.

The selected option is shown by black blob in the middle.

Drop-down lists

Click here...

If a slot has a down arrow button on its right, click the button to drop down a list.

Click on an item in the list to select.

... to select from the list

These two are selected

This one please

Context menus

If you click the right button on almost any object on screen in Windows XP, a short menu will open beside it. This contains a set of commands and options that can be applied to the object.

What is on the menu depends upon the type of object and its *context* – hence the name. Two are shown here to give an idea of the possibilities.

Properties

Most menus have a **Properties** item. The contents of its dialog box also vary according to the nature of the object. For shortcuts, like the one for QuickTime shown below, there is a *Shortcut* panel that controls the link to the program. The (hidden) *General* panel has a description of the file – this panel is in every file's Properties box.

Files can be opened, sent to a removable disk or off in the mail, and deleted – amongst other things.

The Clock can be adjusted, and as it is on the Taskbar, you can also arrange the screen display from this menu.

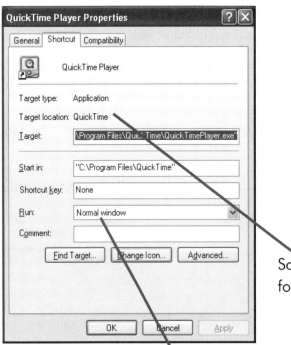

Some properties are there for information only ...

... others can be changed

The Start menu

Take note

Windows uses *'document'* to mean any file created by any application. A word-processed report is obviously a document, but so is a picture file from a graphics package, data files from spreadsheets, video clips, sound files – any file produced by any program.

Clicking on **start** at the bottom left of the screen opens the Start menu.

At the top left are links to your **browser** and **e-mail** software (normally Internet Explorer and Outlook Express, but see page 85).

Beneath these are links to your **most-used programs** – initially this will be empty.

At the bottom left is the **All Programs** link (see the next page).

At the top right are links to **My Documents** and other folders where documents are commonly stored.

My Recent Documents holds a list of your latest documents. Selecting one from this list will run the relevant application and open the file for you to work on (see page 10).

You can configure your PC through the **Control Panel** (Chapter 7), and the **Printers and Faxes** (Chapter 8).

Help and Support starts the Help system (Chapter 2).

Use **Search** to track down files on your computer, or to find Web pages or people on the Internet.

Log off… allows the current user to stop using the PC – and for a new user to start – without turning it off.

Turn Off Computer is the only safe way to shut down the PC.

My Start menu – yours will be different as the menu automatically adapts to your usage and can also be customised by you – see Chapter 6

Running a program

The programs already on your PC, and virtually all of those that you install later, will have an entry in the **All Programs** menu. Selecting one from here will run the program, ready for you to start work.

A program can also be run by selecting a document that was created by it. Links to the documents used most recently are stored in the **My Recent Documents** folder.

- ❑ Running a program
- 1 Click 🏳 start .
- 2 Point to Programs.
- 3 Point to the menu that contains the program – you may have to point to the next menu level.
- 4 Click on the name to run the program.
- ❑ From Documents
- 5 Click 🏳 start .
- 6 Point to My Recent Documents.
- 7 Click on the file to get started on it.

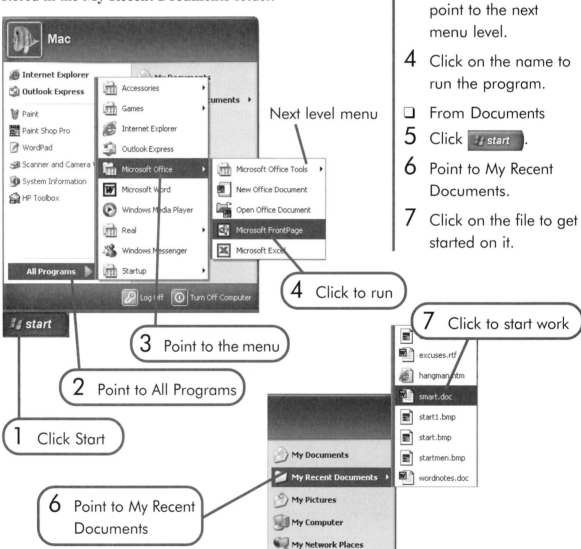

Next level menu

4 Click to run

3 Point to the menu

2 Point to All Programs

1 Click Start

7 Click to start work

6 Point to My Recent Documents

Logging off and on

Basic steps

❏ Logging off

1 Click **start**.

2 Click Log Off.

3 If you want to leave your programs active, to return to later, select Switch User.

4 If you have finished work, select Log Off.

❏ Logging on

5 Switch on the PC.

6 Click on your user name.

7 If you have created a password, type it in.

Windows XP is designed to be a multi-user system. It can be used for networks (see Chapter 10), or can allow several users to share one PC safely (see *User Accounts*, page 132).

Users must 'log on' at the start of a session, to gain access to their folders and settings. When they have finished they should either turn off (see page 12) or 'log off', to protect their area from damage – accidental or otherwise – by other users.

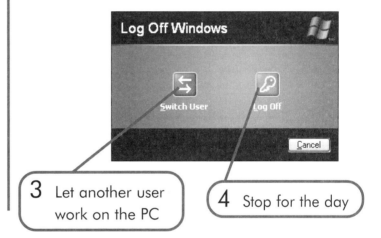

> **3** Let another user work on the PC

> **4** Stop for the day

> **6** Click on your name

> **7** Type the password if required

Shutting down

When you have finished work on your computer, you must shut it down properly, and not just turn it off. This is essential. During a working session, application programs and Windows XP itself may have created temporary files – and any data files that you have been editing may still be open in memory and not yet written safely to disk. A proper shutdown closes and stores open files and removes unwanted ones.

Restart

The Turn off computer dialog box offers a **Restart** option. You may need this after installing new software or hardware. It is also one way to solve problems – see opposite for more on this.

There will probably also be a **Stand By** or **Hibernate** option. This will turn off the main power-using parts of your system – the hard drive, monitor and fans – but leave the RAM memory active, and files and programs open, keeping track of what you were doing, so that you can start up quickly when you return.

Systems differ – check your PC's handbook to find out about its stand by facilities.

See opposite

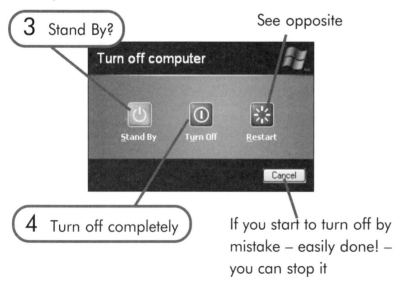

3 Stand By?

Turn off computer

Stand By   Turn Off   Restart

Cancel

4 Turn off completely

If you start to turn off by mistake – easily done! – you can stop it

Basic steps

1 Click start .

2 Select Turn Off Computer.

3 Click Stand By if you want to get back to work quickly later in the day.

4 Click Turn Off if you have finished work completely.

Take note

If you simply turn off the PC, or have to use the Restart button, when it starts up again, Windows will offer to check your hard drive(s) in case there is a problem. The check only takes a few moments and is normally worth doing.

Basic steps

❏ Misbehaving program

1 Open the program's File menu and select Exit (or Close) – saving files if prompted.

2 Restart the program.

❏ Hung system

3 Press [Control] + [Alt] + [Delete] together.

4 At the Task Manager dialog box, select the one marked 'not responding' and click .

5 Restart the program.

❏ Dead keyboard

6 Press the Restart button on front of the PC.

Take note

Windows XP grew out of NT/2000, and most applications written for those will work reliably on XP. Applications written for Windows 95/98/Me are more likely to either not work, or to be unstable.

Coping with crashes

Windows XP is a pretty stable system, but things do go wrong. A 'crash' can can be at several levels.

● A program may simply misbehave – it will still run, but not respond or update the screen correctly. Close it – saving any open files – and run it again. If it still behaves badly, close down all your programs and restart the PC.

● The system will 'hang' – i.e. nothing is happening and it will not respond to the mouse or normal keyboard commands. If the **[Control]** + **[Alt]** + **[Del]** keystroke works, you can reach the Task Manager to close the offending application, which may get things moving again.

● You get a total lock up where it will not pick up **[Control]** + **[Alt]** + **[Del]**. Press the little restart button on the front of the PC. It is there for just these times!

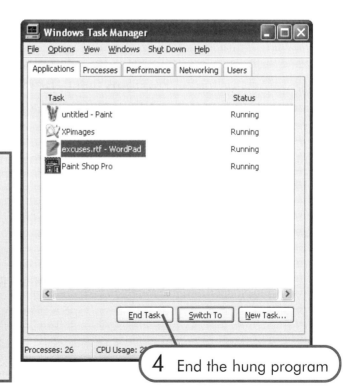

4 End the hung program

Summary

❏ Windows is an intuitive system – if something *feels* right, it probably *is* right.

❏ All Windows software works in much the same way, so once you have got the hang of one program, you are half way to learning the next.

❏ The mouse is an important tool. Practise using it – a good excuse for playing the games!

❏ Some operations are easier with keys, and just a few can only be done from the keyboard.

❏ Selections can usually be made by picking from a list or clicking on a button or check box.

❏ Every object has a context menu containing those commands that you may want to use with it.

❏ The Start button is the main way into the system. Get to know your way around its menus.

❏ Applications can be run directly from the quick links to programs or the All Programs menu, or through documents in folders or in the My Recent Documents list.

❏ You must Turn Off or Log Off properly at the end of a work session.

❏ You may have to restart the system after installing new kit or to recover from a program crash.

❏ You can break into a hung program and start the Task Manager by pressing [Control] + [Alt] + [Del].

2 Help!

Help with applications 16

Finding Help 20

Help and support 22

Instant Help 26

Summary 28

Help with applications

All modern Windows applications have the same style of Help system. Older Windows programs had a slightly different system.

You can get Help in several ways:

● Use the Help menu on applications and accessories;

● Click **?** for 'query' Help on dialog boxes.

● Press **[F1]** – anywhere, any time – to get into the Help system.

In all application Help systems there are three approaches:

● an organised **Contents** list;

● **Index**ed Help pages;

● a word-based **Search** facility.

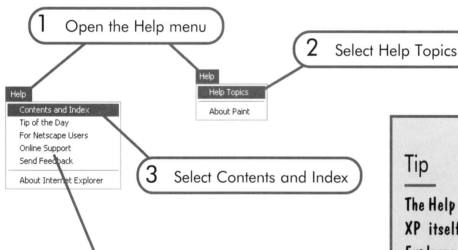

1 Open the Help menu

2 Select Help Topics

Help
Contents and Index
Tip of the Day
For Netscape Users
Online Support
Send Feedback
About Internet Explorer

Help
Help Topics
About Paint

3 Select Contents and Index

Most applications today also offer additional support through the Internet

Tip

The Help system in Windows XP itself and in Windows Explorer is slightly different from that in applications – see pages 22 to 25.

Basic steps

1 Click the Contents tab if this panel is not at the front already.

2 Click on a ● icon or its text to see the page titles – or the next level of books.

3 Click on a ? icon or its text to read a page.

4 Click on Related Top-ics to reach any linked pages

5 Click ☒ to exit Help.

The Toolbar

Hide Closes the tabs and is replaced by **Show** to reopen them.

Back Return to previous Help page.

Forward On to next (visited) Help page.

Options For keyboard users – can be opened by [Alt]+[O].

Web Help Link to Microsoft Web site.

Contents

This approach treats the Help pages as a book. You scan through the headings to find a section that seems to cover what you want, and open that to see the page titles. (Some sections have sub-sections, making it a two or three-stage process to get to page titles.)

Some Help pages have Related topics links to take you on to further pages.

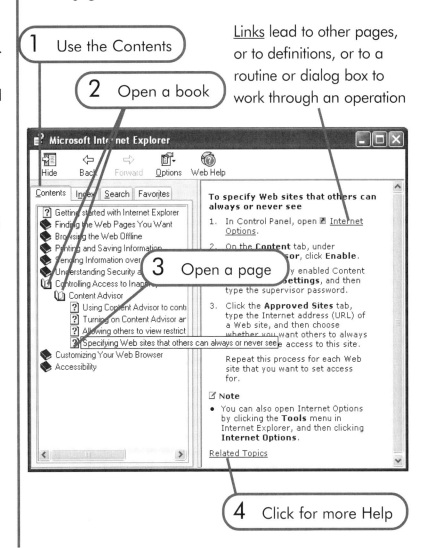

1 Use the Contents

2 Open a book

Links lead to other pages, or to definitions, or to a routine or dialog box to work through an operation

3 Open a page

4 Click for more Help

Using the Index

Though the Contents are good for getting an overview of how things work, if you want help on a specific problem – usually the case – you are better off with the Index.

This is organised through an cross-referenced list of terms. The main list is alphabetical, with sub-entries, just like the index in a book. And, as with an index in a book, you can plough through it slowly from the top, or skip through to find the words that start with the right letters. Once you find a suitable entry, you can display the list of cross-referenced topics and pick one of those.

Basic steps

1 Click the Index tab.

2 Start to type a word into the slot then scroll to the topic.

3 Select an Index entry.

4 Click [Display].

5 Pick a topic from the Topics Found list.

6 Click [Display].

❑ If there is only one relevant topic page, the system will take you directly to it after Step 4.

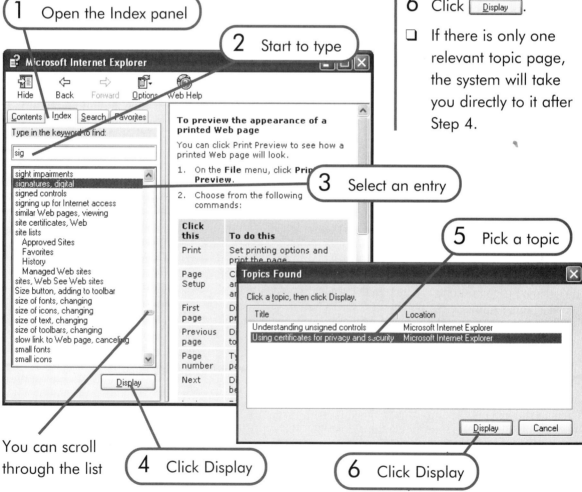

1 Open the Index panel

2 Start to type

3 Select an entry

5 Pick a topic

You can scroll through the list

4 Click Display

6 Click Display

Search for Help

1 Click the Search tab.
2 Type a keyword into the slot.
3 Click [List Topics].
4 Pick a topic from the list.
5 Click [Display].

On the Index panel you are hunting through the titles of Help pages. On the Search panel, the system looks for matching *keywords* within pages.

● A keyword can be any word which might occur in the pages that you are looking for.

● If you give two or more, the system will only list pages which contain all those words.

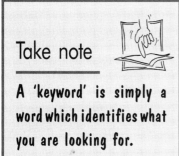

Take note

A 'keyword' is simply a word which identifies what you are looking for.

Tip

Sometimes the screen is not redrawn properly after displaying the definition of an underlined term. Use Options > Refresh to re-store the display.

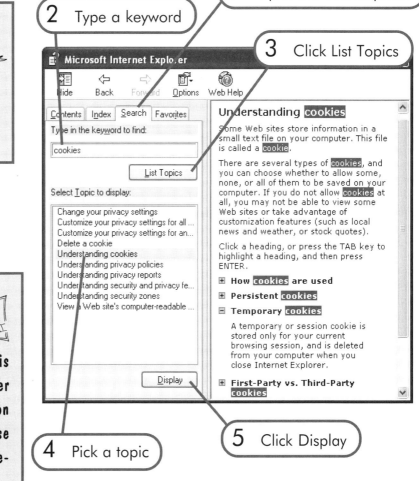

1 Open the Search panel

2 Type a keyword

3 Click List Topics

4 Pick a topic

5 Click Display

Finding Help

In older Windows applications you will meet this in place of the Search panel. It is based on the same principles – searching for matching words within Help pages – but is used in a slightly different way.

Basic steps

1   Open the Find panel.

2   Type your word into the top slot. As you type, words starting with the typed letters appear in the pane beneath.

3   If you want to narrow the search, go back to Step 2, type a space after your first word and give another.

4   Select the most suit-able matching word from the list to narrow the search.

5   Select a topic from the lower pane.

6   Click Display .

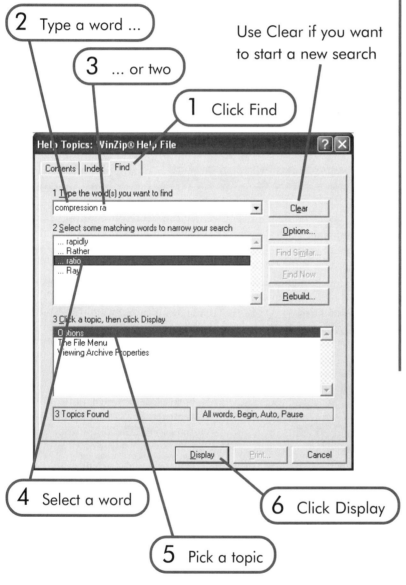

2   Type a word ...

3   ... or two

Use Clear if you want to start a new search

1   Click Find

4   Select a word

6   Click Display

5   Pick a topic

Take note

The first time you use Find for any application, a Wizard will run to create the word list. Take the Minimum option – it will do what you want.

Basic steps

1 On the Find panel, click [Options...].

2 Select All the words... where you are using several words to focus on one topic.

3 Select At least one... where you are giving alternatives, hoping that it recognises one.

4 Decide when you want the system to Begin searching.

5 Click [OK].

Find options

There are several Options that you can set to alter the nature of the search or narrow its scope.

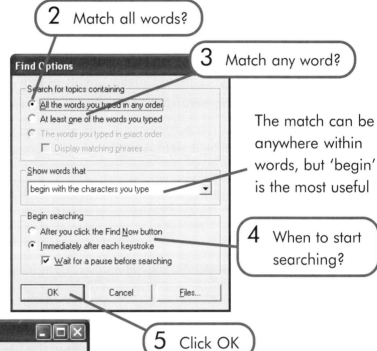

2 Match all words?

3 Match any word?

The match can be anywhere within words, but 'begin' is the most useful

4 When to start searching?

5 Click OK

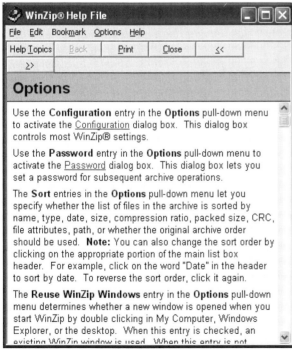

Options

Use the **Configuration** entry in the **Options** pull-down menu to activate the Configuration dialog box. This dialog box controls most WinZip® settings.

Use the **Password** entry in the **Options** pull-down menu to activate the Password dialog box. This dialog box lets you set a password for subsequent archive operations.

The **Sort** entries in the **Options** pull-down menu let you specify whether the list of files in the archive is sorted by name, type, date, size, compression ratio, packed size, CRC, file attributes, path, or whether the original archive order should be used. **Note:** You can also change the sort order by clicking on the appropriate portion of the main list box header. For example, click on the word "Date" in the header to sort by date. To reverse the sort order, click it again.

The **Reuse WinZip Windows** entry in the **Options** pull-down menu determines whether a new window is opened when you start WinZip by double clicking in My Computer, Windows Explorer, or the desktop. When this entry is checked, an existing WinZip window is used. When this entry is not

Older applications display Help pages in a separate window. With these, use Contents or Search to return to the main panel if you need more Help. The illustration comes from WinZip, a program that compresses and uncompresses files – an essential tool for anyone who intends to get material off the Internet. Find out more about it on the Web at http://www.winzip.com.

Help and Support

Windows XP has its own special Help and Support system. It's very comprehensive and has some excellent features, but – most unhelpfully – it looks and feels different from the standard application Help systems. Much the same range of facilities are there, but with new names.

The Home page is the equivalent to Contents. Start to browse through the Help pages from here. It will normally take you four clicks to get from a main topic heading on the Home page, through to a specific page on a Help topic.

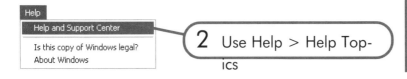

Basic steps

1 Click **start** and select Help.

Or

2 In My Computer or Windows Explorer, use Help > Help and Support Center.

3 Pick a topic from the list on the left.

4 At the next level, click ⊞ by a heading to open a list of topics.

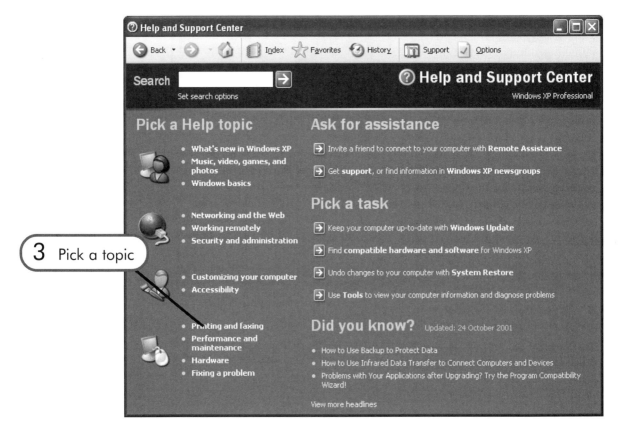

5 Click a sub-topic to display a list of Help pages.

6 Click on a Fix a problem or Pick a task link to open its page.

Click to return to the Home page

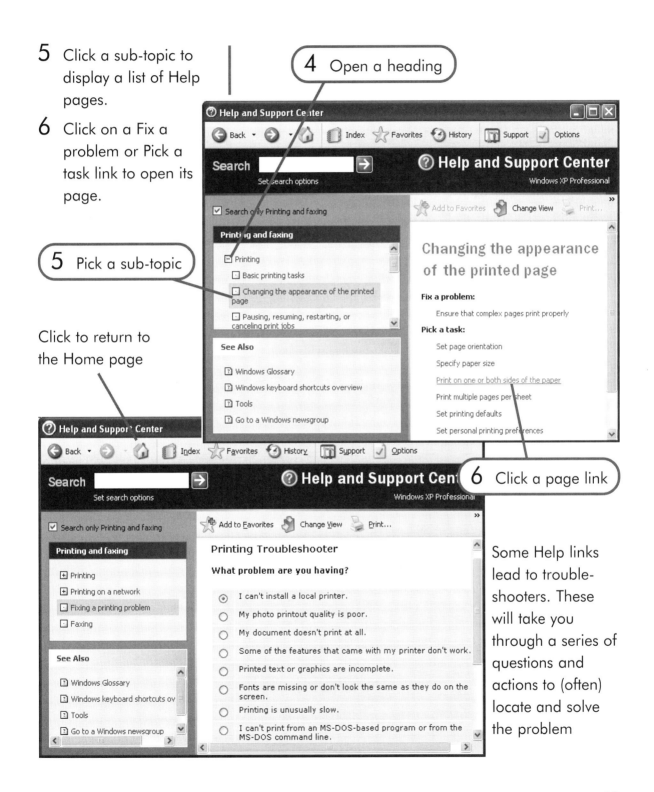

4 Open a heading

5 Pick a sub-topic

6 Click a page link

Some Help links lead to trouble-shooters. These will take you through a series of questions and actions to (often) locate and solve the problem

Help Index

This is almost identical to the Index part of the standard Help systems. Scroll through the index or enter the first few letters to jump to the right part of the list.

Change view

In any part of the Help system, once you have opened a Help page in the right-hand pane, you can use Change View to shrink the display so that only the Help page is visible.

Basic steps

1 Switch to the Index.

2 Start to type a word, then scroll to the topic.

3 Select an Index entry.

4 Click ⬚Display⬚ – you may have a choice of several Help pages.

5 Click Change View to shrink the display – click again to restore the full view if needed.

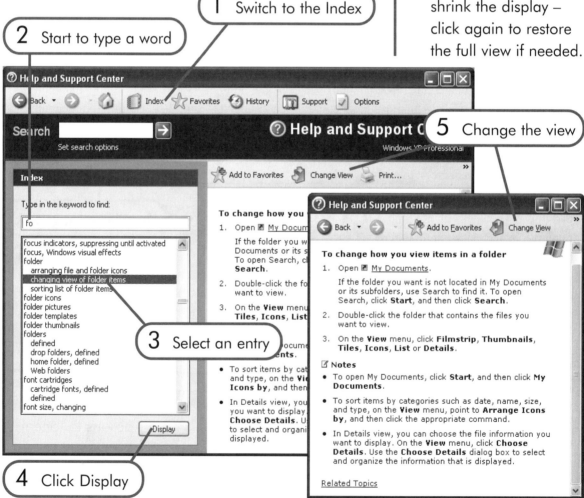

Basic steps

1 Type a keyword into the Search box.

2 Click 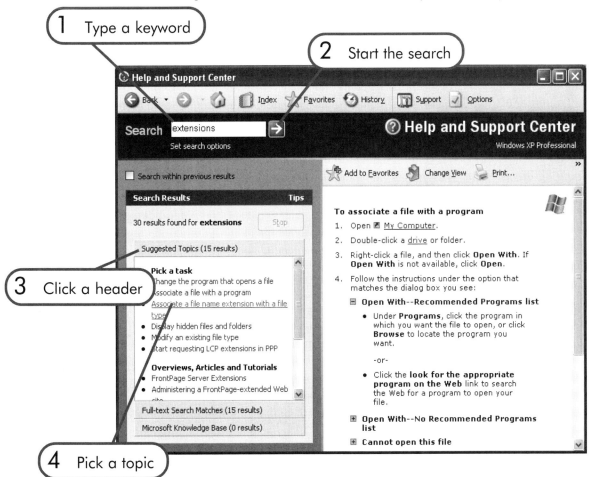.

3 Click on a header to open its set of links.

4 Pick a Help page from the list.

Searching for Help

The **Search** box is present on every page of the Help system. The results are grouped in three sets – click the headers to see their results:

● **Suggested Topics** are normally the most useful. These are the pages that have been indexed by the keyword;

● **Full-text Search Matches** are pages which contain your keywords, but these may only be passing references;

● **Microsoft Knowledge Base** draws help from Microsoft's Web site and is, of course, only available if you are online.

1 Type a keyword

2 Start the search

3 Click a header

4 Pick a topic

Instant Help

As well as the main Help system, Windows XP and Windows applications offer a couple of other useful forms of Help.

The query icon

All dialog boxes and panels in Windows XP and its components – and in any new or recent Windows applications – have an ⚆ icon on the top right of the status bar. You will also find an ⚆ icon on the toolbar of some applications. They can both be used for finding out more about objects on screen.

Basic steps

1 Click on the ⚆ or ⚆ icon.

2 Click the ↘? cursor on the button, option or other item that you want to know about.

3 After you have read the Help box, click anywhere to close it.

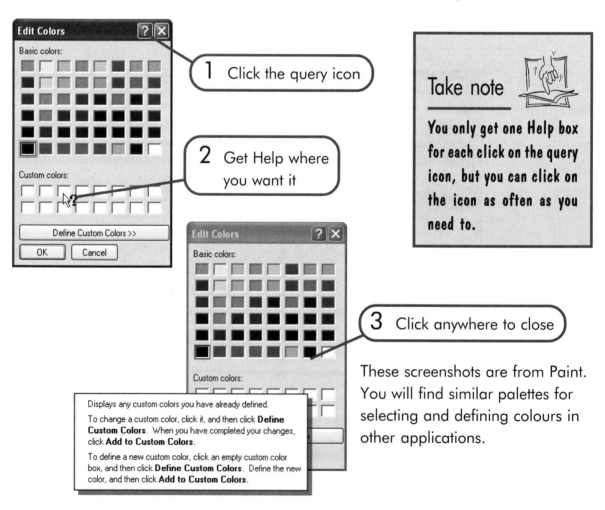

1 Click the query icon

2 Get Help where you want it

3 Click anywhere to close

Take note

You only get one Help box for each click on the query icon, but you can click on the icon as often as you need to.

Displays any custom colors you have already defined.

To change a custom color, click it, and then click **Define Custom Colors**. When you have completed your changes, click **Add to Custom Colors**.

To define a new custom color, click an empty custom color box, and then click **Define Custom Colors**. Define the new color, and then click **Add to Custom Colors**.

These screenshots are from Paint. You will find similar palettes for selecting and defining colours in other applications.

Help on icons

Icons are supposed to be self-explanatory, but their purpose cannot always be summed up in a small image. Never fear, help is near!

Let the cursor rest over an icon for a moment and a label will pop up to tell you what it is. If that isn't enough to tell you what it does, at least you have a name to look up in the Help Index.

Point and wait to see the icon's label

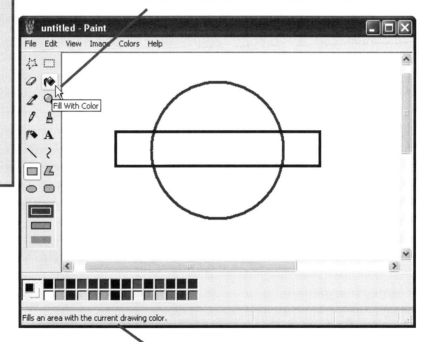

There's more help in the Status Bar

Tip

Even if the Help box doesn't give you enough information, it will give you the words you need to find more detailed Help. From the example on the right, we can get 'Fill', and using that in a Search gets us to detailed instructions on how to fill shapes with colour.

Take note

If a window is in Restore mode — i.e. smaller than the full screen (see page 32 for more) — the message area in the Status Bar may not be long enough to display the Help message in full.

Summary

- ❑ Help is always available.

- ❑ Use the Contents panel when you are browsing to see what topics are covered.

- ❑ Use the Index to go directly to the help on a specified operation or object.

- ❑ If you can't locate the Help in the Index, use the Search (Windows XP) or Find (older Windows applications) facility to track down the pages.

- ❑ Windows XP has a comprehensive – if a little slow – Help and Support system. This has its own special style and approach.

- ❑ For Help with items in a dialog box or panel, click the query icon and point to the item.

- ❑ If you hold the cursor over an icon, a brief prompt will pop up to tell you what it does. There will also be a Help message in the Status Bar.

3 Window control

The window frame 30

Window modes 32

Arranging windows 34

Moving windows 36

Changing the size 37

Scrolling 38

Closing windows 39

Summary 40

The window frame

This is more than just a pretty border. It contains all the controls you need for adjusting the display.

Frame edge

This has a control system built into it. When a window is in Restore mode – i.e. smaller than full-screen – you can drag on the edge to make it larger or smaller (see *Changing the size*, page 37).

Title bar

This is to remind you of where you are – the title bar of the active application (the one you are using) is blue; the bars of other open applications are grey. The bar is also used for moving the window. Drag on this and the window moves (see *Moving windows*, page 36).

Maximize, Minimize and Restore

These buttons change the display mode. Only one of Maximize and Restore will be visible at any one time (see *Window modes*, page 32).

Close

One of several ways to close a window and the program that was running in it (see *Closing windows*, page 39).

Control menu icon

There is no set image for this icon, as every application has its own, but clicking on whatever is here will open the Control menu. This can be used for changing the screen mode or closing the window (see *Window modes*, page 32). Double-clicking this icon will close down the window.

Take note

Most applications can handle several documents at once, each in its own window. These are used in almost the same way as program windows. The applications usually have a **Window** menu containing controls for the document windows.

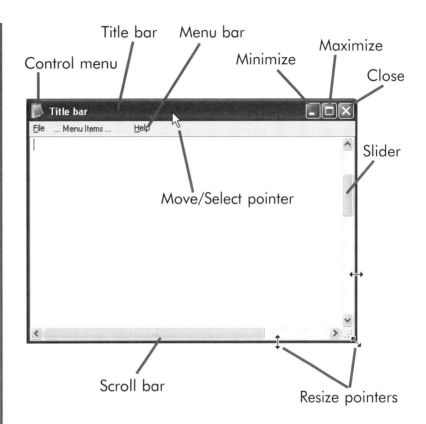

Menu bar

Immediately below the Title bar in an application's window is a bar containing the names of its menus. Clicking on one of these will drop down a list of commands.

Scroll bars

These are present on the right side and bottom of the frame if the display contained by the window is too big to fit within it. The **Sliders** in the Scroll bars show you where your view is, relative to the overall display. Moving these allows you to view a different part of the display. (See *Scrolling*, page 38.)

Window modes

All programs are displayed on screen in windows, and these can normally have three modes:

- Maximized – filling the whole screen;
- Minimized – not displayed, though still present as a button on the Task bar;
- Restore – adjustable in size and in position.

Take note

Some applications run in small, fixed-size windows, so Maximize and Restore do not apply to them.

Maximized

In Restore mode

Minimize

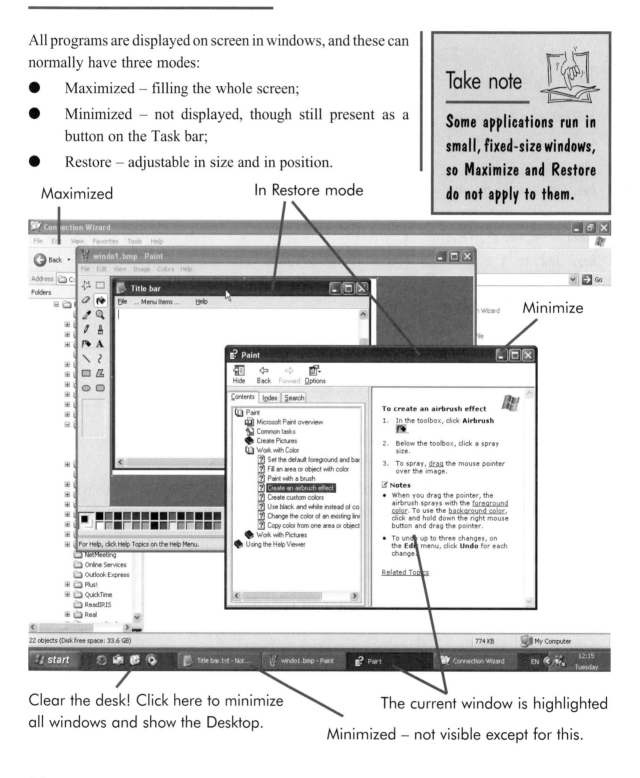

Clear the desk! Click here to minimize all windows and show the Desktop.

The current window is highlighted

Minimized – not visible except for this.

Basic steps

❏ To make a window full-screen

Click  or select Maximize from the Control menu

❏ To shrink a window to an icon

Click 🔲 or select Minimize from the Control menu

❏ To restore a window to variable size

Click 🗗 or select Restore from the Control menu

Changing display modes

Clicking on the buttons in the top right corner of the frame is the simplest way to switch between **Maximize** and **Restore** modes, and to **Minimize** a window. If you prefer it can be done using the Control menu.

The Control menu

Click the icon at the top left to open this. Options that they don't apply at the time will be 'greyed out'. The menu here came from a variable size window. One from a full-screen window would have **Move**, **Size** and **Maximize** in grey.

🗗 Restore	
Move	
Size	
━ Minimize	
🗖 Maximize	
✕ Close	Alt+F4

Using the Taskbar

Click a program's button to bring its window to the top.

Right-click the button to open its Control menu.

Right-click for the menu

Left-click to activate

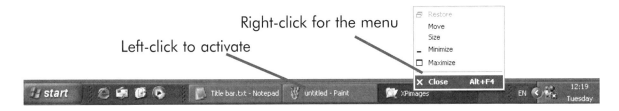

Keyboard control

[Alt]+[Space] opens the Control menu of an application.

[Alt]+[-] (minus) opens the Control menu of a document.

Minimized documents

When you minimize a document window, within an application, it shrinks to a tiny title bar, with just enough room for a name and the icons. Click **Maximize** or **Restore** to open it out again.

Restore   Maximize

Arranging windows

If you want to have two or more windows visible at the same time, you will have to arrange them on your desktop. There are Windows tools that will do it for you, or you can do it yourself.

If you right-click the Taskbar, its menu has options to arrange the windows on the desktop. Open it and you will see **Cascade Windows**, **Tile Windows Vertically** and **Tile Windows Horizontally**. Similar options are on the Window menu of most applications, though these only affect the layout *within* the programs.

Cascade places the windows overlapping with just the title bars of the back ones showing. You might just as well Maximize the current window, and use the Taskbar buttons to get to the rest.

Either of the Tile layouts can be the basis of a well-arranged desktop.

1 Maximize or Restore the windows that you want to include in the layout. Minimize those that you will not be using actively.

2 Right-click the Taskbar to open its menu.

3 Select Tile Windows Horizontally or Tile Windows Vertically.

4 If you only want to work in one window at a time, Maximize it, and Restore it back into the arrangement when you have done.

Tip

If you want to adjust the balance of the layout, you can move and resize the windows.

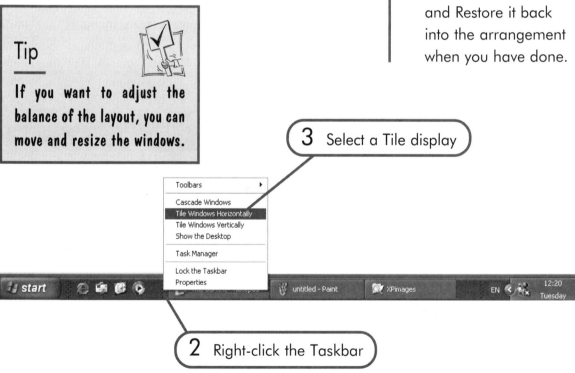

3 Select a Tile display

Toolbars
Cascade Windows
Tile Windows Horizontally
Tile Windows Vertically
Show the Desktop
Task Manager
Lock the Taskbar
Properties

start   untitled - Paint   XPimages   EN   12:20 Tuesday

2 Right-click the Taskbar

Tile

Tip

Cascade works better than Tile on small screens.

Tile arranges open windows side by side (Vertical), or one above the other (Horizontal) – with more than three windows, the tiling is in both directions. As the window frames take up space, the actual working area is significantly reduced. Obviously, larger, high-resolution screens are better for multi-window work, but even on a 1024 x×768 display you cannot do much serious typing in a tiled window.

The Taskbar menu now has an Undo Tile option to restore your screen to its previous state.

Tip

It is generally simplest to work with the active window Maximized and any others Minimized out of the way.

Moving windows

When a window is in **Restore** mode – open but not full screen – it can be moved anywhere on the screen.

● If you are not careful it can be moved almost off the screen! Fortunately, at least a bit of the title bar will still be visible, and that is the handle you need to grab to pull it back into view.

1 If the title bar isn't highlighted, click on the window to make it the active one.

2 Point at the title bar and hold the left button down.

3 Drag the window to its new position – you will only see a grey outline moving.

4 Release the button.

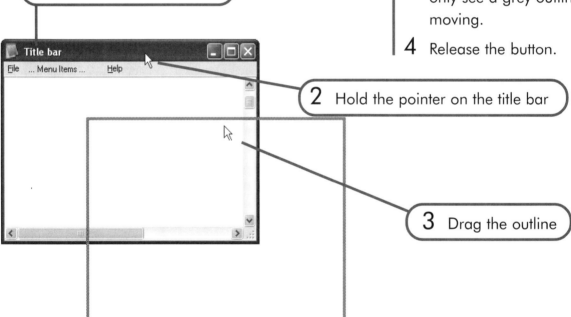

1 Make the window active

Title bar

File ... Menu Items ... Help

2 Hold the pointer on the title bar

3 Drag the outline

4 Release to drop into its new position

36

Basic steps

1 Move the pointer to the edge or corner that you want to pull in or out.

2 When you see the double-headed arrow, hold down the left mouse button and drag the outline to the required size.

3 Release the button.

When a window is in Restore mode, you can change its size and shape by dragging the edges of the frame to new positions.

Combined with the moving facility, this lets you arrange your desktop exactly the way you like it.

● The resize pointers only appear when the pointer is just on an edge, and they disappear again if you go too far. Practise! You'll soon get the knack of catching them.

You can drag any edge or corner

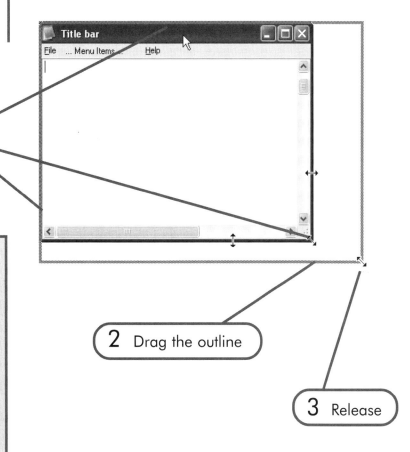

2 Drag the outline

3 Release

Tip

The quickest way to get a window the right size, in the right place, is to use the bottom right size handle to set the shape, then drag the window into position.

Scrolling

What you can see in a window is often only part of the story. The working area of the application may well be much larger. If there are scroll bars on the side and/or bottom of the window, this tells you that there is more material outside the frame. The scroll bars let you pull some of this material into view.

Tip

If a window is blank — and you think there should be something there — push the sliders to the very top and left. That's where your work is likely to be.

Basic scrolls

❑ Drag the slider ▮ to scroll the view in the window. Drag straight along the bar or it won't work!

❑ Click an arrow ▲ to edge the slider towards the arrow. Hold down for a slow continuous scroll.

❑ Click on the bar beside the Slider to make it jump towards the pointer.

Sliders

Arrow buttons

Working area

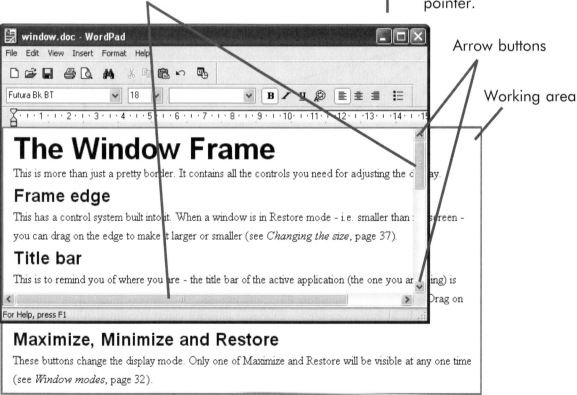

Maximize, Minimize and Restore

These buttons change the display mode. Only one of Maximize and Restore will be visible at any one time (see *Window modes*, page 32).

Basic steps

- Closing an active window

1 Click ❌ or press [Alt]+[F4].

- Closing from the Taskbar

2 Right-click the program's Taskbar button to get its menu.

3 Select Close.

4 If you have forgotten to save your work, take the opportunity that is offered to you.

When you close a window, you close down the program that was running inside it.

If you haven't saved your work, most programs will point this out and give you a chance to save before closing.

There are at least five different ways of closing. Here are the simplest three:

- If the window is in Maximized or Restore mode, click the close icon at the top right of the Title bar. (If your mouse control is not too good, you may well do this when you are trying to Maximize the window!)

- If the window has been Minimized onto the Taskbar, right-click on its button to open the Control menu and use **Close**.

- If you prefer working from keys, press **[Alt]+[F4]**.

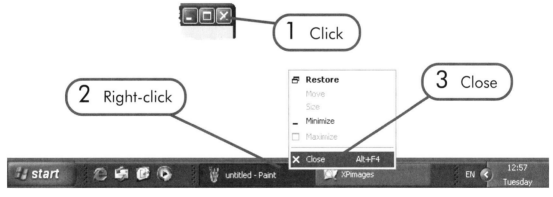

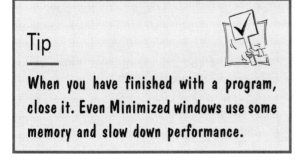

Tip

When you have finished with a program, close it. Even Minimized windows use some memory and slow down performance.

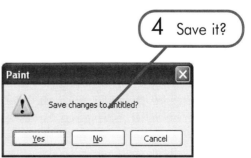

Summary

❑ Use the controls in the window frame to adjust the window display.

❑ You can move between windows by clicking on any visible part of them – though the active parts of the frame should be avoided.

❑ Windows can be displayed in Maximized (full-screen) or Restore (variable size) modes, or Minimized to icons.

❑ Minimized windows can be restored to full size by clicking on their icon in the Taskbar.

❑ Windows can be arranged on the desktop by picking Cascade or Tile from the Taskbar menu.

❑ A window can be moved about the screen by dragging on its title bar.

❑ You can change the size of a window (in Restore mode) by dragging on any of its edges.

❑ The scroll bars will let you move the working area inside a window.

❑ Closing a window closes its program.

4 Exploring folders

The four faces of Explorer 42

Files and folders 43

Windows Explorer 46

My Computer 47

Customizing the toolbar 51

Folder Options 52

Expanding folders 54

Creating a folder 56

Moving folders 58

Deleting folders 59

Summary 60

The four faces of Explorer

Windows XP has one file management application, but with four very distinct faces. Whichever one you start from, it can be changed into any other by altering the display or by switching the focus between your computer, your network and the Internet.

Windows Explorer (page 46)

This has a dual display, with the folder structure on the left and the contents of the current folder on the right. It can access the folders in all of the drives attached to your computer, and any that may be accessible to you over a network. Windows Explorer is a good tool for moving files between folders.

My Computer (page 47)

In this mode, the folder structure display is replaced by a panel containing sets of commonly used tasks – the sets vary, depending upon what's selected at the time. When first opened it gives an overview of the components of your own system. You can then open another window to get a detailed look at folders in a drive, and continue opening further windows to go deeper into folders. My Computer only shows the contents of one folder, but you can have as many My Computer windows open as you need.

My Network Places

This is the same as My Computer, but opens with the focus on the networked machines.

Internet Explorer (Chapter 12)

This is the mode for exploring the Internet. The main differences are that it displays Web content and the toolbar has a slightly different selection of tools.

Take note

Which display you use for your file management is up to you. I prefer to see the folder structure for most jobs – certainly for organising files and folders – but I use the simpler, My Computer/My Network Places displays when I'm simply looking to see what's where or if I need two folders open at once to compare their contents.

Tip

The Desktop icon **My Documents** simply opens My Computer at the My Documents folder.

Files and folders

- ❏ Root – the folder of the disk. All other folders branch off from the root.

- ❏ Parent – a folder that contains another.

- ❏ Child – a sub-folder of a Parent.

- ❏ Branch – the structure of sub-folders open off from a folder.

Tip

When planning the folder structure, keep it simple. Too many folders within folders can make it hard to find files.

If you are going to work successfully with Windows – or any computer system – you must understand how its disk storage is organised, and how to manage files efficiently and safely. In this chapter, we will look at the filing system, working with folders and the screen displays of Explorer and My Computer. In later sections, we will cover managing files and looking after your disks.

Folders

The hard disks supplied on modern PCs are typically 10 gigabytes or larger. 1 Gigabyte is 1 billion bytes and each byte can hold one character (or part of a number or of a graphic). That means that a typical hard disk can nearly to 2 billion words – enough for about 10,000 hefty novels! More to the point, if you were using it to store letters and reports, it could hold many, many thousands of them. Even if you are storing big audio or video files you are still going to get hundreds of them on the disk. It must be organised if you are ever to find your files.

Folders provide this organisation. They are containers in which related files can be placed to keep them together, and away from other files. A folder can also contain sub-folders – which can themselves by subdivided. You can think of the first level of folders as being sets of filing cabinets; the second level are drawers within the cabinets, and the next level divisions within the drawers. (And these could have subdividers – there is no limit to this.)

Don't just store all your files in My Documents – it will get terribly crowded! Have a separate folder for each type of file, or each area of work (or each user of the computer), subdividing as necessary, so that no folder holds more than a few dozen files.

Paths

The structure of folders is often referred to as the **tree**. It starts at the **root**, which is the drive letter – C: for your main hard disk – and branches off from there.

A folder's position in the tree is described by its **path**. For most operations, you can identify a folder by clicking on it in a screen display, but now and then you will have to type its path. This should start at the drive letter and the root, and include every folder along the branch, with a backslash (\) between the names.

For example:

C:\DTP

C:\WORDPROC\LETTERS

When you want to know a path, look it up in the Explorer display and trace the branches down from the root.

Filenames

A filename has two parts – the name and an extension.

The **name** can be as long as you like, and include almost any characters – including spaces. But don't let the freedom go to your head. The longer the name, the greater the opportunity for typing errors. The most important thing to remember when naming a file is that the name must mean something to you, so that you can find it easily next time you come back to the job.

The **extension** can be from 0 to 3 characters, and is separated from the rest of the name by a dot. It is used to identify the nature of the file. Windows uses the extensions COM, EXE, SYS, INI, DLL to identify special files of its own – handle these with care!

Most applications also use their own special extensions. Word-processor files are often marked with DOC; spreadsheet files are usually XLS; database files typically have DB extensions.

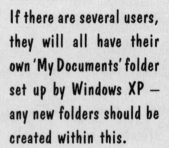

Take note

If there are several users, they will all have their own 'My Documents' folder set up by Windows XP – any new folders should be created within this.

If you are saving a file in a word-processor, spreadsheet or other application, and are asked for a filename, you normally only have to give the first part. The application will take care of the extension. If you do need to give an extension, make it meaningful. BAK is a good extension for backup files; TXT for text files.

When an application asks you for a filename – and the file is in the *current* folder – type in the name and extension only. If the file is in *another* folder, type in the path, a backslash separator and then the filename.

For example:

MYFILE.DOC

C:\WORPROC\REPORTS\MAY25.TXT

A:\MYFILE.BAK

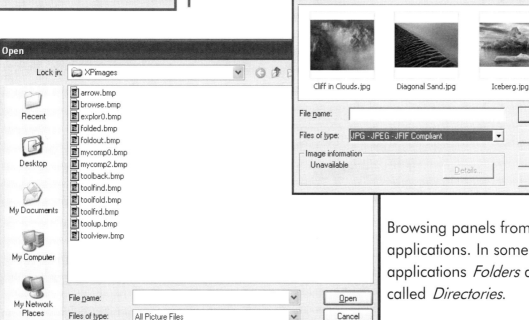

Browsing panels from two applications. In some older applications *Folders* are called *Directories*.

45

Windows Explorer

In the Explorer window, the main working area is split, with folders in the Explorer Bar, and the contents on the right.

The **Folder List** may show the disk drives and first level of folders only, but folders can be expanded to show the sub-folders (see *Expanding folders*, page 54).

The **Contents** shows the files and sub-folders in the currently selected folder. These can be displayed as thumbnails, tiles, icons or with details of the file's size, type and date it was last modified (see *Arranging icons*, page 62).

The **Status Bar** shows information about the selected file(s) or folders.

The **Toolbar** has the buttons for the most commonly-used commands. Other can be added, if desired (see page 51).

The **Explorer Bar** can also be used to display Common Tasks (see opposite), Search (see page 70), Favorites (see page 168) or History (see page 167).

□ Starting Explorer
1 Click start.
2 Point to All Programs then to Accessories.
3 Click Windows Explorer.
4 Click on a folder's icon □ or its name to open it and display its contents.

Click to close the Explorer Bar

Contents – here shown in Icon View

Explorer bar, displaying the Folder List

Current folder

First level folder

Sub-folder

Status Bar

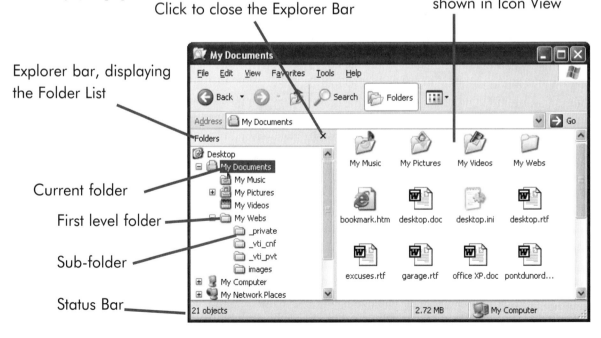

46

The Standard toolbar

My Computer

Back ▾ Go back to previous folder

➡ ▾ Go to next folder

↗ Go to parent folder

🔍 Search Search for files (page 70)

📂 Folders Switch between Folder List and Common Tasks

▦ ▾ Alternative views of files (page 48)

There are three key differences between Windows Explorer and My Computer:

- My Computer opens with a view of the whole PC, rather than in *My Documents*.

- Instead of the Folder List, the Explorer bar shows **Common Tasks** – these vary, depending upon what is selected in the Contents pane.

- The Status Bar is turned off by default.

Any or all of these can be changed.

Click to expand/collapse the display of items

The Status bar has been turned back on here

Use the drop-down list to switch to drives or folders higher up the same path

Tip

Remember that My Computer and Windows Explorer are the same program and can be used and customized in the same ways.

Display options

The display options can be set from the View menu and the Views button. These options can be set at any time, and can be different for different folders. There are two areas of choice.

Which toolbars to you want?

- The **Standard** is pretty well essential.

- The **Address** is useful. Its drop-down outline of the folder structure offers a quick way to move between drives.

- The **Links** carries quick links to selected Web sites.

Alternative Views

- **Filmstrip** is only available in folders that have been customized for pictures (see Tip opposite). It shows a large image of the selected file, with the rest in a strip across the bottom (example, page 50).

- **Thumbnails** show little previews of files, if possible. Graphics and Web pages will be displayed, and Word, PowerPoint and Excel documents will display if they were saved with a preview (example, page 50).

- **Tiles** shows a large, easy to recognise icon, accompanied by key details of the file (example, page 49).

- **Icons** (example, page 46) and **List** (example, page 54) show lots of files in little space.

- **Details** shows – and can be sorted on – the name, type, size and date of files (example, page 62).

Tip

There's more on arranging files in Chapter 5.

Basic steps

- ❑ Displaying Toolbars

1 Open the View menu.

2 Point to Toolbars then click on a toolbar to turn it on or off.

- ❑ Icons and lists

3 Open the View menu.

or

4 Click .

5 Choose a view.

Common file icons

 Bitmap image

GIF image

Web page

Text

Word document

Excel workbook

O Open Type font

System file – handle with care!

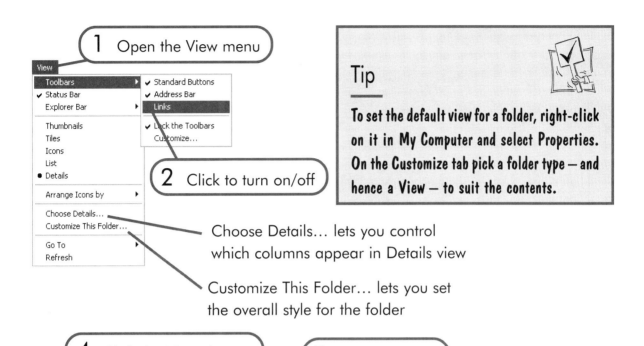

1 Open the View menu

2 Click to turn on/off

Tip

To set the default view for a folder, right-click on it in My Computer and select Properties. On the Customize tab pick a folder type — and hence a View — to suit the contents.

Choose Details… lets you control which columns appear in Details view

Customize This Folder… lets you set the overall style for the folder

4 Click the Views button

5 Choose a view

This is Tiles View

Filmstrip view
The size of the
main image
depends upon
the size of the
window

Rotate left/right

Next/previous

Thumbnail view
Good for images,
Web pages and
Office files

Customizing the toolbar

1 Right-click on the toolbar and select Customize…

2 To add a button – or a separator – select it from the Available list and click `Add ->`.

3 To remove a button, select it from the Current list and click `<- Remove`.

4 To adjust its position, select it and click `Move Up` (left) or `Move Down` (right).

5 Set the Text and Icon options as required.

6 Click `Close`.

The contents of the Standard toolbar are not fixed. You can add or remove buttons, move them around within the bar, and adjust their appearance. This is all done through the **Customize Toolbar** dialog box.

There are buttons available for most of the other commands in the menus, including Cut, Copy, Paste, Copy To Folder and Move To Folder (all from the Edit menu) which can be used for copying and moving files and folders, instead of dragging.

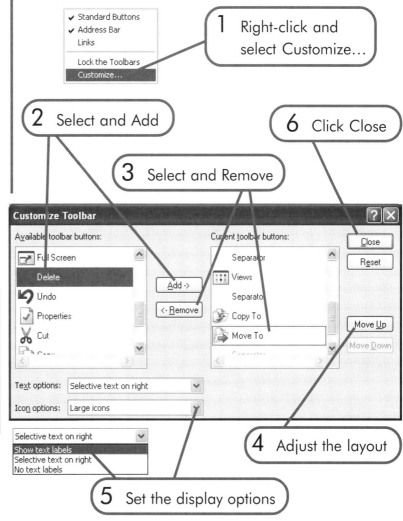

1 Right-click and select Customize…

2 Select and Add

6 Click Close

3 Select and Remove

4 Adjust the layout

5 Set the display options

Tip

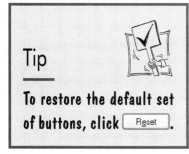

To restore the default set of buttons, click `Reset`.

Folder Options

These control the overall appearance of folders and the way that files are handled.The dialog box has four tabs.

On the **General** tab there are three options:

- Select **Show common tasks in folders** to enable them – the actual display is toggled by the Folders button.

- You can open each folder in a new or in the same window.

- You can select items with a single or double-click.

The **View** panel controls the display of files. There are two main options here. The first is whether to show 'hidden' files. These are mainly found in the *Windows* and *Windows/System* folders and are ones that you do not usually need to see and which are safer out of the way.

- **Application extensions** – files with **.DLL** extensions. They are used by applications and must not be deleted.

- **System files** – marked by **.SYS** after the name. These are essential to Windows' internal workings.

- **Drivers** – with **.VXD** or **.DRV** extensions. These make printers, screens and other hardware work properly.

The second key choice is whether you want to set different display styles for different folders – turn on *Remember each folder's view settings* if you do. If you have a mixture of styles already and want all folders to look the same, you can use the buttons to make them all look like the current folder or reset them all to their default settings.

The **File Types** tab is used to link programs and documents. We'll come back to this on page 77.

The **Offline Files** tab is for use where files are stored on a network. The tab's options are not normally active on a single PC.

1 Open the Tools menu and select Folder Options...

2 On the General panel select whether or not to Show common tasks in folders.

3 Set the Browse Folders option – the same or a new window?

4 Set the Click option.

5 Go to the View panel.

6 Click the checkbox to turn options on or off.

7 Click [Apply] to test the effect.

8 When you have done. click [OK].

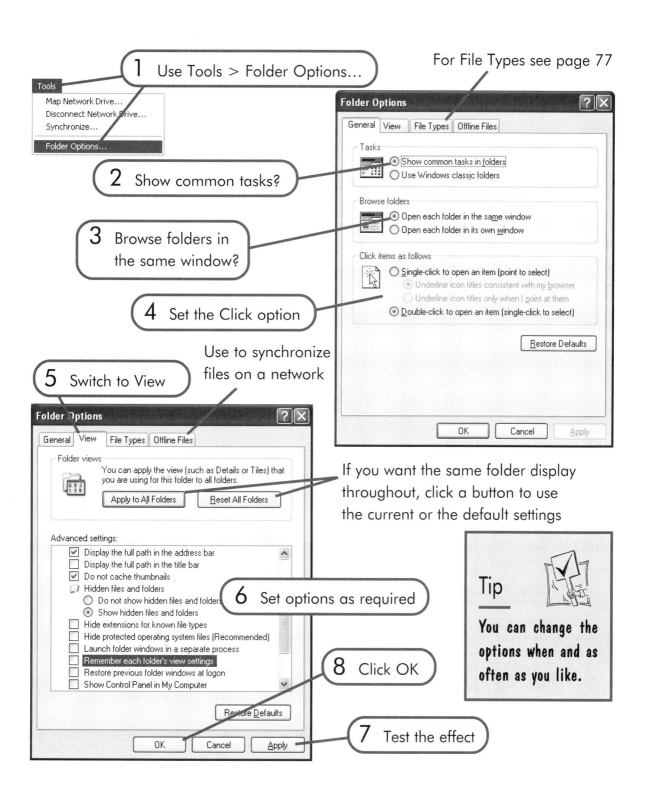

1 Use Tools > Folder Options...

Tools
Map Network Drive...
Disconnect Network Drive...
Synchronize...
Folder Options...

For File Types see page 77

Folder Options ？☒

General | View | File Types | Offline Files

Tasks
- ⦿ Show common tasks in folders
- ◯ Use Windows classic folders

2 Show common tasks?

Browse folders
- ⦿ Open each folder in the same window
- ◯ Open each folder in its own window

3 Browse folders in the same window?

Click items as follows
- ◯ Single-click to open an item (point to select)
  - ⦿ Underline icon titles consistent with my browser
  - ◯ Underline icon titles only when I point at them
- ⦿ Double-click to open an item (single-click to select)

Restore Defaults

4 Set the Click option

Use to synchronize files on a network

5 Switch to View

OK   Cancel   Apply

Folder Options ？☒

General | View | File Types | Offline Files

Folder views
You can apply the view (such as Details or Tiles) that you are using for this folder to all folders.

Apply to All Folders   Reset All Folders

If you want the same folder display throughout, click a button to use the current or the default settings

Advanced settings:
- ☑ Display the full path in the address bar
- ☐ Display the full path in the title bar
- ☑ Do not cache thumbnails
- Hidden files and folders
  - ◯ Do not show hidden files and folders
  - ⦿ Show hidden files and folders
- ☐ Hide extensions for known file types
- ☐ Hide protected operating system files (Recommended)
- ☐ Launch folder windows in a separate process
- ☐ Remember each folder's view settings
- ☐ Restore previous folder windows at logon
- ☐ Show Control Panel in My Computer

6 Set options as required

Restore Defaults

OK   Cancel   Apply

8 Click OK

7 Test the effect

Tip

You can change the options when and as often as you like.

53

Expanding folders

The *Folders* structure can be shown in outline form, or with some or all of its branches shown in full. The best display is always the simplest one that will show you all you need. This usually means that most of the structure is collapsed back to its first level of main folders, with one or two branches expanded to show particular sub-folders. It is sometimes worth expanding the whole lot, just to get an idea of the overall structure and to see how sub-folders fit together.

If a folder has sub-folders, it will have a symbol beside it.

    ☐   has sub-folders, and can be expanded

    ☐   sub-folders displayed and can be collapsed.

- ❑ To expand a folder
1 Click ⊞ by its name.
2 Click ⊞ by any sub-folders if you want to fully expand the whole branching set.

- ❑ To collapse a folder
3 Click ⊟ by its name.
- ❑ To collapse a whole branch
4 Click ⊟ by the folder at the top of the branched set.

1 Expand folder

4 Collapse whole set

3 Collapse folder

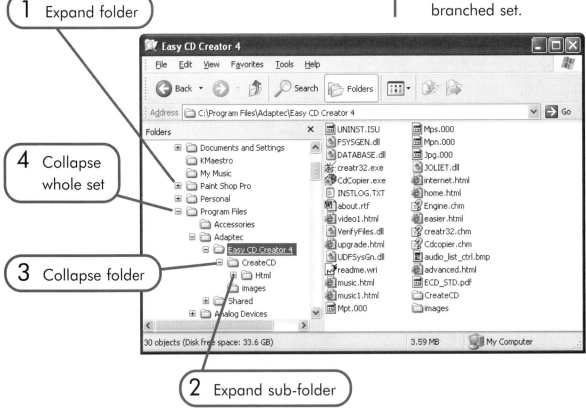

2 Expand sub-folder

Basic steps

1 Right-click on the folder name and select Properties.

2 Check the size totals.

3 Switch to Customize.

4 Select a folder type to suit its contents.

5 Click Choose Picture and browse for a decorative picture.

6 Click 🗙 to close the Properties panel.

Folder properties

Expanding a folder will show you what is in it, but not how much space all its files and sub-folders occupy. The space report in the Status bar tells you how much is used by the files in the current folder only – not in its sub-folders. The total space figure can be important if you want to back up the folder, or copy it to floppies. The Properties panel will tell us this.

On the Customize tab you can set the folder type, which determines the default view, and add a picture to the front of the folder, or change its icon, if you like.

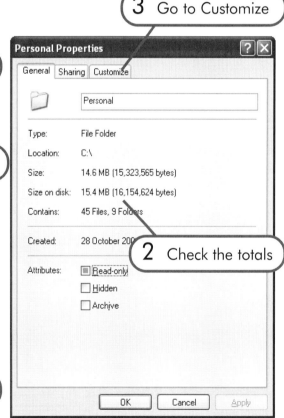

3 Go to Customize

6 Close

2 Check the totals

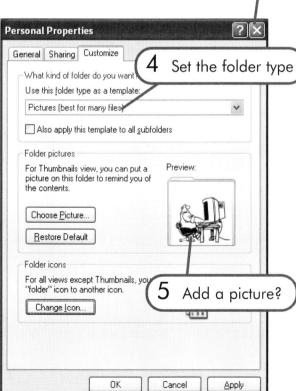

4 Set the folder type

5 Add a picture?

The size on disk is more than the size of the files, because some space is left empty but unusable at the ends of files

Creating a folder

Organised people set up their folders before they need them, so that they have places to store their letters – private and business, reports, memos, notes, and whatever, when they start to write them on their new system. They have a clear idea of the structure that they want, and create their folders at the right branches.

1   Select the folder that will be the parent of your new one, or the root if you want a new first-level folder.

2   Open the File menu and point to New then select Folder.

3   Replace 'New Folder' with a new name – any length, any characters, as with filenames.

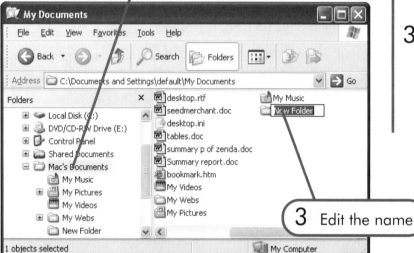

1   Click on the parent

3   Edit the name

2   Select File > New > Folder

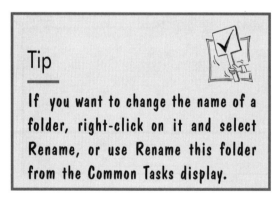

Tip

If you want to change the name of a folder, right-click on it and select Rename, or use Rename this folder from the Common Tasks display.

Your folder structure

Tip

When adding new software, let the setup program put it where it wants. As long as the system knows where the program files are, you don't have to worry about it!

How you organise your folders is entirely up to you, but these guidelines may help.

If several people use the same computer, they should each have their own user account (see page 132), which will give them their own 'My Documents' folder. This can be subdivided as required to match their interests.

Don't have too many levels of sub-folders – it gets confusing. Create your main folders in My Documents, or at the C: drive if you are the PC's only user, and aim for no more than two levels of sub-folders within these. It's a pain having to work through four or five levels to reach stuff!

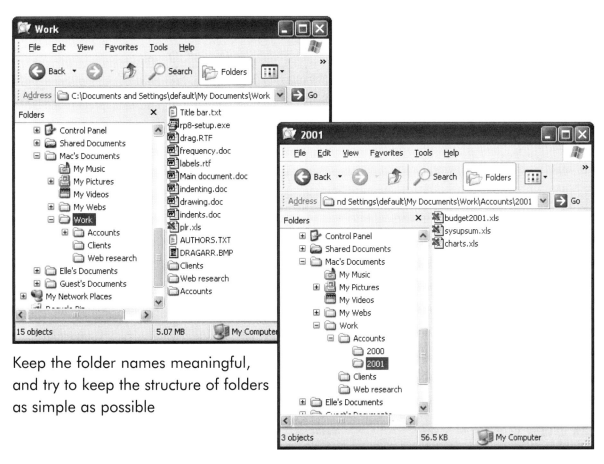

Keep the folder names meaningful, and try to keep the structure of folders as simple as possible

Moving folders

Those of us who are less organised set up our new folders when the old ones get so full that it is difficult to find things. Nor do we always create them in the most suitable place in the tree. Fortunately, Windows XP caters for us too. Files can easily be moved from one folder to another (see *Moving and copying*, page 66), and folders can easily be moved to new places on the tree.

Here, *Web pix* is being moved from within my *Work* folder into *Shared Pictures*, so that others can access it.

1 Arrange the display so that you can see the folder you want to move and the place it has to move to.

2 Drag the folder to its new position – the highlight will show you which one is currently selected.

Tip

Copying a folder – and all its files – to another disk can be a quick way to make a backup of a set of files.

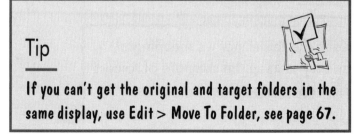

Tip

If you can't get the original and target folders in the same display, use Edit > Move To Folder, see page 67.

Deleting folders

1 Select the folder.

2 Check the files list. Are there any there? Do you want any of them? No, then carry on.

3 Right-click on the folder to open the context menu or open the File menu and select Delete.

4 If necessary, you can stop the process by clicking No when you are asked to confirm that the folder is to be thrown in the Bin.

This is not something you will do every day, for deleting a folder also deletes its files, and files are usually precious things. But we all acquire programs we don't need, keep files long past their use-by dates, and sometimes create unnecessary folders.

● Don't worry about accidental deletions – files and folders deleted from your hard disk can be restored thanks to the Recycle Bin (see page 69).

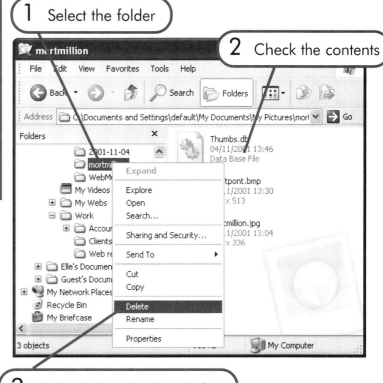

1 Select the folder

2 Check the contents

3 Right-click and select Delete

4 Confirm or stop

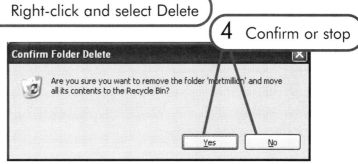

Tip

You can also delete folders or files by dragging them directly to the Recycle Bin.

59

Summary

❑ Windows Explorer, My Computer and My Network Places are faces of the same program and are used for managing your files and folders.

❑ Disks are normally subdivided into folders, to give organised storage for files.

❑ A folder's place in the system is identified by its path.

❑ A filename has two components, the name and an extension. The name can be as long as you like, and contain any mixture of letters, digits and symbols. Extensions are used to identify the nature of the file.

❑ The Toolbar gives you quick access to all the commonly-used commands. You can add or remove buttons as required.

❑ You can select which toolbars to show and which view to use for displaying the files.

❑ You can control the file displays through the Folder options.

❑ Those files that are essential to the system are usually hidden from view. They can be brought into view, but should always be treated with respect.

❑ When you create a new folder, it will be placed on the branch below the selected folder.

❑ Try to keep your folder structure as simple as possible – you are going to have to find your way around your system!

❑ A folder, and its files, can be deleted or moved to a new position in the structure.

5 Managing files

Arranging icons 62

Selecting sets of files 64

Moving and copying 66

Deleting files 68

The Recycle Bin 69

Finding files 70

Properties 72

Shortcuts 74

File Types 77

Summary 78

Arranging files

Unless you specify otherwise, folders and files are listed in alphabetical order. Most of the time this works fine, but when you are moving or copying files, or hunting for them, other arrangements can be more convenient.

1   Open the View menu and point to Arrange Icons By.

2   Select Name, Size, Type, or Modified (date).

❑   Details View

3   Open the View menu and select Details.

4   To sort by Name, Size, Type or Date, click on the column header. Click again to sort into reverse order.

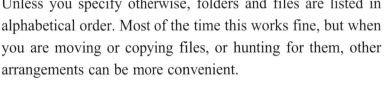

1   Open View – Arrange Icons

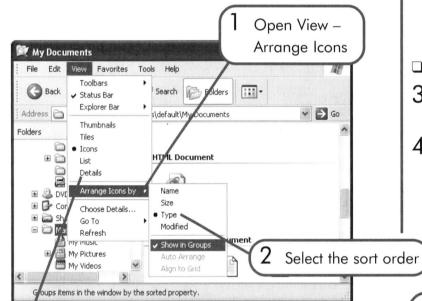

2   Select the sort order

3   Use View > Details

4   Click the header to sort on that column

Tip

If you have a lot of files in a folder, turn on **Show in Groups** to make them easier to handle. The option works in all Views, except **List**.

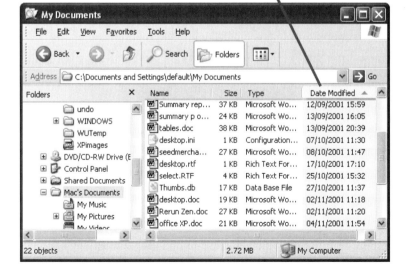

Basic steps

❏ Adjusting Details

1 Point the cursor at the dividing line between two field headings.

2 When the cursor changes to ↔, drag the dividing line to change the width of the field on its left.

❏ Adjusting the split

3 Point anywhere on the bar between the panes to get the ↔ cursor.

4 Drag the shadowed line to adjust the relative size of the panes.

Improving visibility

The amount of information in a My Computer or Windows Explorer display can vary greatly, depending upon the number of items in a folder and the display style. You should be able to adjust the display so that you can see things properly.

As well as being able to set the overall size of the window, you can also adjust the width of each field in a Details display, and the split between the Folders and Contents panes of Explorer.

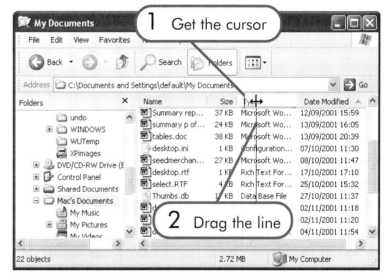

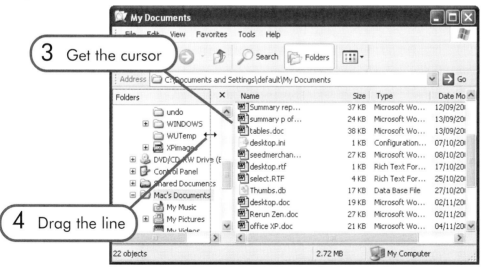

Selecting sets of files

You can easily select one file by clicking on it, but you can also select sets of files. This is useful when you want to back up a day's work by copying the new files to a floppy, or move a set from one folder to another or delete a load of unwanted files.

You can select:

● a block of adjacent files;

● a scattered set;

● the whole folder-full.

The same techniques work with all display styles.

Basic steps

❑ To select a block using the mouse

1 Point to one corner of the block and click.

2 Drag an outline onto the ones you want.

❑ [Shift] selecting

3 Click on the file at one end of the block.

4 If necessary, scroll the window to bring the other end into view.

5 Hold [Shift].

6 Click on the far end file.

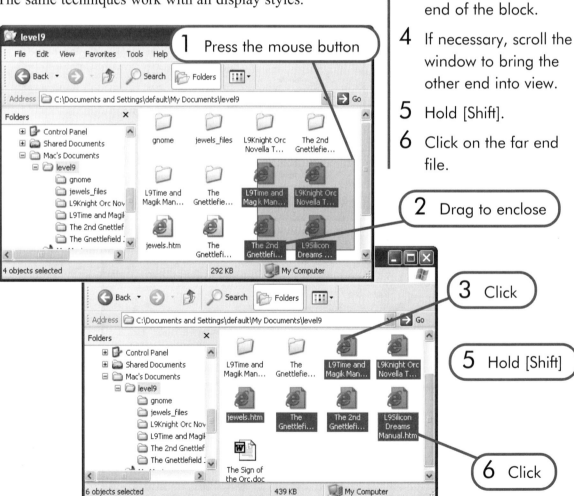

64

Basic steps

❑ To select scattered files

1 Click on any one of the files you want.

2 Hold [Control] and click each of the other files.

❑ You can deselect any file by clicking on it a second time.

❑ To select all the files

3 Open the Edit menu.

4 Choose Select All.

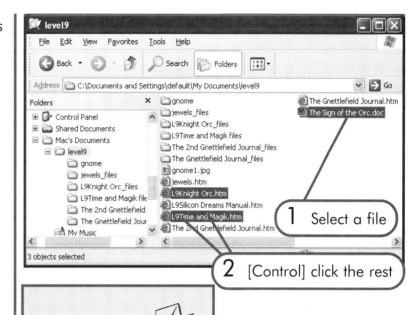

1 Select a file

2 [Control] click the rest

Tip

It may be easier to arrange icons by Name, Date or Type, then [Shift] select.

3 Open the Edit menu

4 Choose Select All

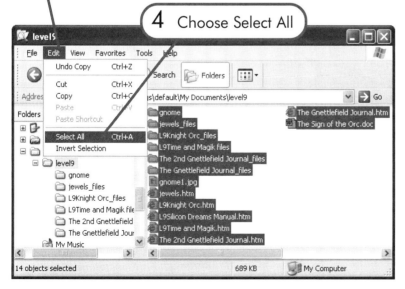

Tip

If you want all the files except for a scattered few, select those few, then use Edit > Invert Selection to deselect them and select the others.

65

Moving and copying

When you drag a file from one place to another, it will either move or copy the file. In general:

● It is a **move** if you drag to somewhere *on the same disk.*

● It is a **copy** if you drag the file *to a different disk.*

When you are dragging files within a disk, you are usually moving to reorganise your storage; and copying is most commonly used to create a safe backup on a separate disk.

If you want to move a file from one disk to another, or copy within a disk, hold down the right mouse button while you drag. A menu will appear when you reach the target folder. You can select **Move** or **Copy** from there.

1 Select the file(s).

2 Scroll the Folders list so that you can see the target folder – don't click on it!

3 Point to any one of the selected files and drag to the target.

or

4 Hold down the right mouse button while you drag then select Move or Copy.

❑ Quick copy to a floppy

5 Right-click on the file to open its context menu, point to Send To and select the floppy drive.

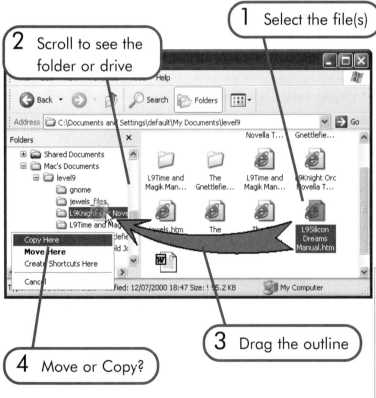

1 Select the file(s)

2 Scroll to see the folder or drive

Copy Here
Move Here
Create Shortcuts Here

Cancel

4 Move or Copy?

3 Drag the outline

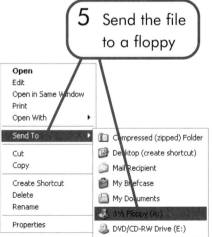

5 Send the file to a floppy

Open
Edit
Open in Same Window
Print
Open With ▶
Send To ▶
Cut
Copy
Create Shortcut
Delete
Rename
Properties

Compressed (zipped) Folder
Desktop (create shortcut)
Mail Recipient
My Briefcase
My Documents
3½ Floppy (A:)
DVD/CD-RW Drive (E:)

Basic steps

1 Select the file(s).
2 Open the Edit menu and select Copy To or Move To Folder.
3 Select the target drive or folder.
4 Click Move or Copy.

Tip

If you like this method of managing files, you can add **Copy To** and **Move To** buttons to the toolbar (see page 51).

Move To Folder/Copy To Folder

If you are having difficulty arranging the Explorer display so that you can see the source files and the target folder, the simplest approach is to use the **Move To Folder** or **Copy To Folder** commands. These let you pick the target folder through a dialog box.

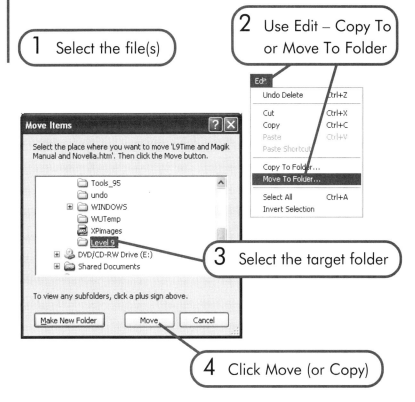

1 Select the file(s)

2 Use Edit – Copy To or Move To Folder

3 Select the target folder

4 Click Move (or Copy)

Cut and Paste

Windows XP allows you to move and copy files and folders – or any other data, through an area of memory called the Clipboard.

Cut, **Copy** and **Paste** are on the **Edit** menu of all Windows applications.

Copy stores a copy of the file or folder in the Clipboard.

Cut removes the original file, storing a copy in the Clipboard.

Paste puts a copy of the stored file into the current folder.

Deleting files

Thanks to the Recycle Bin, deleting files is no longer the dangerous occupation that it used to be – up to a point! Anything that you delete from the hard disk goes first into the Bin, from which it can easily be recovered. Floppies are different. If you delete a file from a floppy it really does get wiped out!

1 Select the file, or group of files.

2 Drag them to the Recycle Bin on the Desktop or in Explorer.

or

3 Press [Delete].

4 At the Confirm prompt, click Yes or No to confirm or stop the deletion.

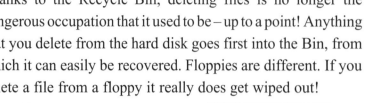

1 Select the files

2 Drag to the Bin

3 Press [Delete]

4 Confirm

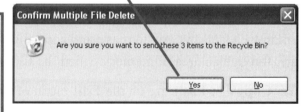

With single deletions, the filename is displayed; with multiple deletions you just get the number of selected files.

Take note

If you want to rename a file, select it and use File > Rename, or click twice, separately, on the filename to highlight it. The name can then be edited or retyped.

Basic steps

Recycle Bin

1 Open the Recycle Bin from the icon on the desktop or from Windows Explorer.

2 Select the files that were deleted by mistake – the Original Location field shows you where they were.

3 Right-click for the context menu and select Restore or click Restore the items in the common tasks.

This is a wonderful feature, especially for those of us given to making instant decisions that we later regret. Until you empty the Bin, any 'deleted' files and folders can be instantly restored – and if the folder that they were stored in has also been deleted, that is re-created first, so things go back into their proper place.

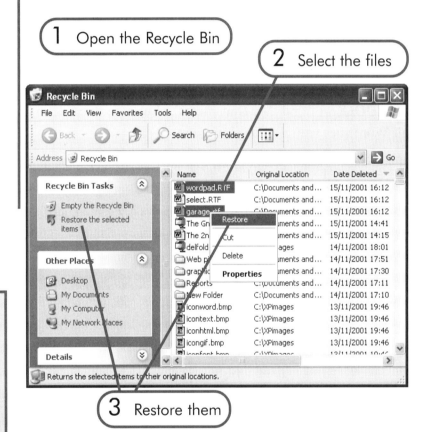

1 Open the Recycle Bin

2 Select the files

3 Restore them

Tip

Files sent to the Recycle Bin stay there until you empty it. Do this regularly, to free up disk space. Check that there is nothing that you want (Restore any files if necessary) then use File > Empty Recycle Bin.

Take note

You cannot open files from within the Recycle Bin – they must be restored if you want to look at them.

Finding files

If you are well organised, have a clear and logical structure of folders and consistently store files in their proper places, you should rarely need this facility. However, if you are like me, you will be grateful for it. You can find files by name, type, age, size or contents.

Partial names and wildcards

If you type part of a name into the name box, the Search will track down any file with those characters anywhere in the name.

e.g. '**DOC**' will find 'My **Doc**uments', 'Letter to **doc**tor', and all Word files with a **.DOC** extension.

If you know the start of the name and the extension, fill the gap with the wildcard ***.** (include the dot!)

e.g. *REP*.TXT* will find '**REP**ORT MAY 15.*TXT*', '**REP**LY TO IRS.**TXT**' and similar files.

1 In My Computer or Windows Explorer, click Search.

2 Select All files or folders.

3 Type as much of the name as you know into the Name slot.

4 If the file can be identified by a word or phrase, enter it.

5 Select the drive from the Look in list.

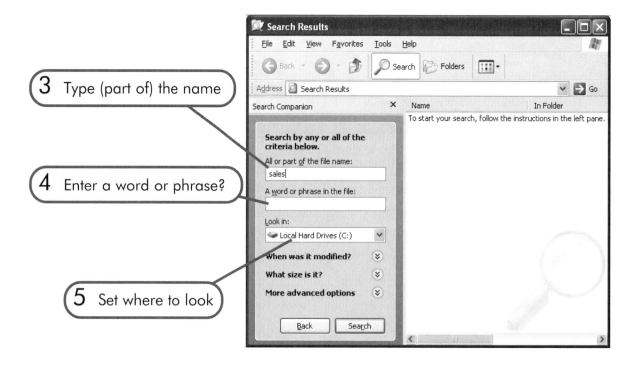

3 Type (part of) the name

4 Enter a word or phrase?

5 Set where to look

6 If you want to narrow the search, you can define when it was modified, its size and other advanced options, including type. Click ⊗ to open an option area and give any known details.

7 Click [Search].

8 Double-click the file to run it or to open it with its linked program.

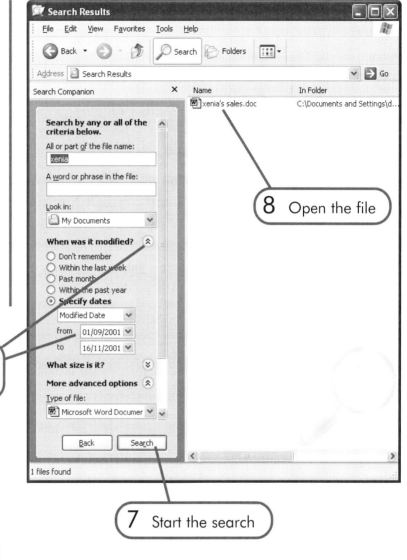

6 Give some details to narrow the search

8 Open the file

7 Start the search

 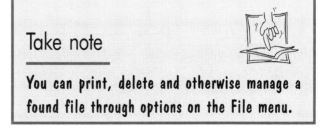

Properties

Everything in Windows XP has Properties. If you open the **Properties** dialog box for any file, you will see a **General** tab, containing information about the file and some controls. Some files have additional tabs.

● Program files have **Version** tabs carrying product details, and **Compatibility** tabs where you can set the program to run in an earlier Windows mode;

● Word-processor, spreadsheet and other data files created by newer applications have **Summary** and **Statistics** tabs. Summary information is created by the user to describe the contents of the file; the Statistics include the number of pages, words, characters and the like, and the dates when the file was created, last modified or accessed.

● Shortcuts have their own special tabs (see next pages).

Basic steps

1 Right-click the file and select Properties from the short menu.

2 If you want to prevent the file from being edited, tick the Read Only checkbox.

3 Click the names to open other tabs, if present.

4 Click [OK] or [X] to close.

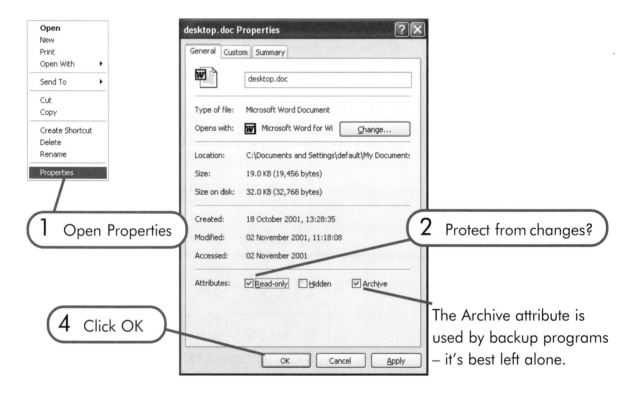

1 Open Properties

2 Protect from changes?

4 Click OK

The Archive attribute is used by backup programs – it's best left alone.

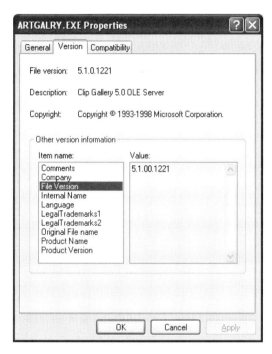

The Version tab (left) can tell you more about when and by whom a program was created. Use it to check which version of a program you have, when reporting bugs or contemplating an update.

The Summary tab (below) displays information written into it while the file was open in its application. This can be edited – click Apply or OK to save the revised information.

Programs have Compatibility tabs – if an older application does not work reliably in XP, try running it in the appropriate compatibility mode

Shortcuts

You can run a program by double-clicking on its EXE file in My Computer, but shortcuts make it easier. Shortcuts can be added to the Start menu (see page 85) or placed on the Desktop – a convenient way of running programs that you use regularly.

Most programs will have shortcuts set up in the Start menu, and sometimes on the Desktop, when they are installed. If not, or you want extra ones, you can set up a shortcut in a minute – and if you don't make much use of it, you can remove it even faster!

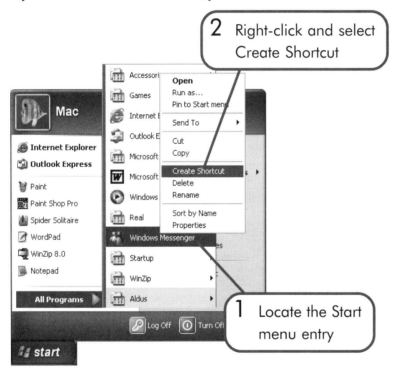

2 Right-click and select Create Shortcut

1 Locate the Start menu entry

1 If the program has a Start menu entry, click **start** and locate it.

2 Right-click on it and select Create Shortcut.

or

3 In My Computer, find the program file – it will have an EXE or COM extension.

4 Right-click on the file and select Send To then Desktop from its context menu.

5 Edit the name – it will be 'Shortcut to...'

❑ Editing Properties

6 Open the icon's Properties box and click the Shortcut tab.

7 Change the Start in folder if required.

Tip

You can also create desktop shortcuts to files or folders, so that you can open them with a single click. Just right-click on them in My Computer and select Send To > Desktop.

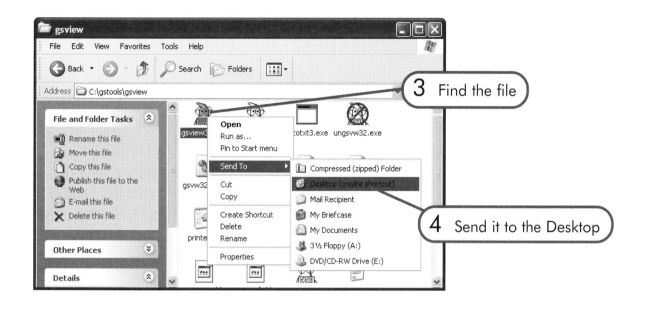

3 Find the file

4 Send it to the Desktop

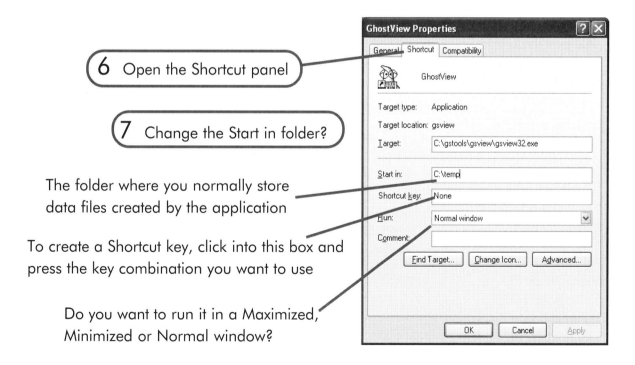

6 Open the Shortcut panel

7 Change the Start in folder?

The folder where you normally store data files created by the application

To create a Shortcut key, click into this box and press the key combination you want to use

Do you want to run it in a Maximized, Minimized or Normal window?

Tidying the Desktop

Too many shortcuts will clutter up your Desktop. Here are two simple ways to cut through the clutter.

- If you don't expect to ever use a shortcut again, select it and press **[Delete]**. Note that this does not remove the program, file or folder – only the shortcut.

- Run the **Desktop Cleanup Wizard**. It will collect unused shortcuts and pack them into a folder. If you decide you need them, you can easily drag them out of the folder.

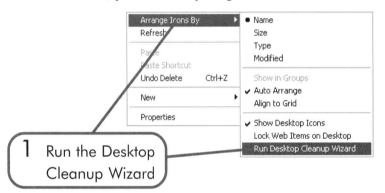

1 Run the Desktop Cleanup Wizard

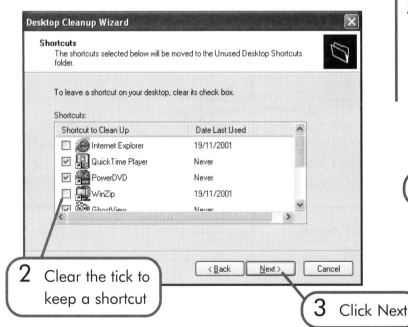

2 Clear the tick to keep a shortcut

3 Click Next

❑ Desktop Cleanup

1 Right-click anywhere on the Desktop, point to Arrange Icons By and select Run Desktop Cleanup Wizard

2 The wizard will have ticked all the unused shortcuts – if there are any you want to retain, clear the ticks.

3 Click [Next >].

4 You will be shown the shortcuts to be re-moved – if you agree, click [Finish].

5 The shortcuts will disappear and a new folder, *Unused Desktop Shortcuts* will be placed on the Desktop.

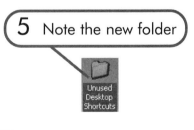

5 Note the new folder

Basic steps

1 Open the Tools menu and select Folder Options...

2 Go to the File Types tab.

3 Select a file type.

4 Click Change... .

5 At the Open With dialog box, select the application and click OK .

6 Click Close .

Windows keeps a list of registered file types. These are ones that it knows how to handle. If you open a document of a known type, the system will run the appropriate application and load in the file. There are some types that Windows doesn't know about and others which you may prefer to open with a different program. The associations are easily made or changed through the **File Types** tab of the **Folder Options** dialog box.

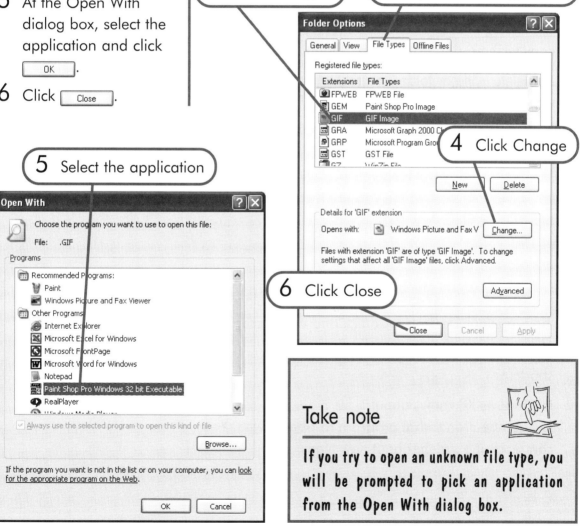

3 Select the type

2 Open the File Types tab

4 Click Change

5 Select the application

6 Click Close

Take note

If you try to open an unknown file type, you will be prompted to pick an application from the Open With dialog box.

Summary

❑ You can arrange icons by Name, Type, Size or Date.

❑ Files and folders can be displayed as icons or in lists with details.

❑ You can use [Shift] to select a block of files, or [Ctrl] to select a scattered set. A block of files can also be selected with the mouse.

❑ Dragging a file will normally move it within the disk, or copy it to a floppy.

❑ By holding the right button as you drag, you can copy within a disk or move to a floppy.

❑ To delete a file or folder, press [Delete]. If the file was on the hard disk, it is sent to the Recycle Bin, from which it can be recovered. Files deleted from a floppy really are deleted.

❑ The Search utility will help you to track down files if you have forgotten where you put them, or what they were called.

❑ The Properties box of a file can be a useful source of information.

❑ You can create Shortcuts to programs and place them on your Desktop for quick and easy access.

❑ Use the Desktop Cleanup Wizard to tidy up unused shortcuts.

❑ If Windows XP knows about a file type, it knows how to describe it and what program to open it with. You can teach the system about new types.

6 The Taskbar

Taskbar options 80

Taskbar toolbars 82

The Start menu 84

Organising the menu 86

Setting the Clock 87

Summary 88

Taskbar options

Many parts of the Windows XP system can be tailored to your own tastes. Some of the most important are covered in the next two chapters. We'll start with the Taskbar and the Start menu. You can adjust the size of the menu icons, turn the clock on or off, hide the Taskbar, or place it on any edge of the screen.

Basic steps

❑ Adjusting the display

1 Right-click on any blank area of the Taskbar.

2 Select Properties from the context menu.

3 Set the options.

4 Click [Apply] to see how they look.

5 Click [OK] to fix the settings and close.

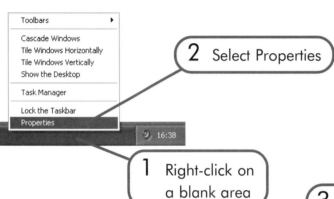

2 Select Properties

1 Right-click on a blank area

3 Set options

Auto-hide slides the Taskbar off-screen when not in use. Point off-screen to restore the Taskbar to view.

Keep the taskbar on top – when off, to see the Taskbar you must minimise applications or press [Ctrl]-[Esc]

Group similar taskbar buttons – if the same program is running in several windows, they can all be stacked onto one button to save space, as in the example here

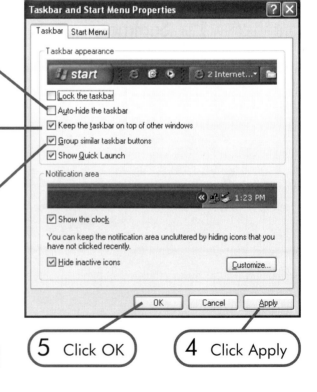

5 Click OK

4 Click Apply

80

Basic steps

Moving and resizing

❑ Moving

1 Point to any free space on the Taskbar.

2 Drag towards the top, left or right of the screen, as desired.

3 Release the mouse button.

❑ Resizing

4 Point to the inside edge of the Taskbar.

5 When the cursor changes to ←→, drag to change the width of the Taskbar.

Moving the Taskbar is quite easy to do by mistake, so it is just as well to know how to do it intentionally – if only to correct a mistake!

Resizing the Taskbar – making it deeper or wider – is sometimes useful. Narrow vertical displays are almost unreadable.

When you are running a lot of programs with a horizontal Taskbar, the titles on the buttons can be very small. If you deepen the display, you get two rows of decent-sized buttons.

Take note

If you like to keep the Taskbar visible, it takes least space at the top or bottom of the screen.

If you have a lot of applications running at once, or several toolbars on the Taskbar (see page 82), then the Taskbar is best at the left or right edge, but with Auto-Hide turned on.

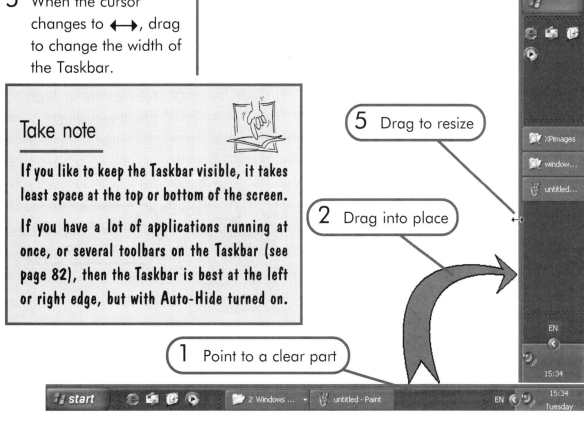

5 Drag to resize

2 Drag into place

1 Point to a clear part

Taskbar toolbars

The normal setting for the Taskbar is to have the Quick Launch and the Language bars, plus buttons for any open applications and the clock.

If you find that you do not use them, these toolbars can be removed, to allow more space for application buttons.

If you like working from the Taskbar, other toolbars can be added, turning the Taskbar into the main starting point for all your commonly-used activities.

❑ Adding toolbars

1 Right-click on an empty place on the Taskbar to open its context menu.

2 Point to Toolbars.

3 Click on a toolbar to add it to (or remove it from) the Taskbar.

❑ Toolbar options

4 Right-click on a toolbar to open its context menu.

5 Point to View and set the button size.

6 Turn on the toolbar Title if required.

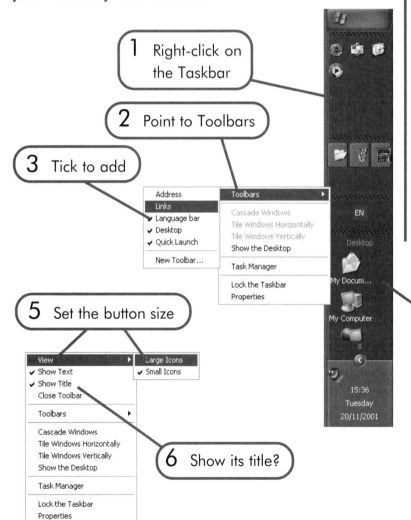

1 Right-click on the Taskbar

2 Point to Toolbars

3 Tick to add

Address		Toolbars ▶
Links		Cascade Windows
✓ Language bar		Tile Windows Horizontally
✓ Desktop		Tile Windows Vertically
✓ Quick Launch		Show the Desktop
New Toolbar...		Task Manager
		Lock the Taskbar
		Properties

5 Set the button size

View ▶	Large Icons
✓ Show Text	✓ Small Icons
✓ Show Title	
Close Toolbar	
Toolbars ▶	
Cascade Windows	
Tile Windows Horizontally	
Tile Windows Vertically	
Show the Desktop	
Task Manager	
Lock the Taskbar	
Properties	

6 Show its title?

4 Right-click on a toolbar

EN

Desktop

My Docum...

My Computer

15:36
Tuesday
20/11/2001

Basic steps

1 Create a new folder –
   it can be in any con-
   venient place.

2 Set up shortcuts to you
   main programs.

3 Open the Taskbar
   menu, point to
   Toolbars and select
   New Toolbar.

4 Select your new folder.

5 Click [OK].

Tip

**If you add toolbars to the
Taskbar, a horizontal display will get too crowded
to see things properly unless you have it more than
one line deep (see the
example below). Other-
wise, drag it to a side
position, make it wide
enough for the buttons to
fit and turn on AutoHide.**

Creating a new toolbar

If you like the Taskbar as a means of starting programs, you can
set up new Taskbar toolbars to hold your own collections of
shortcuts to programs that you use regularly.

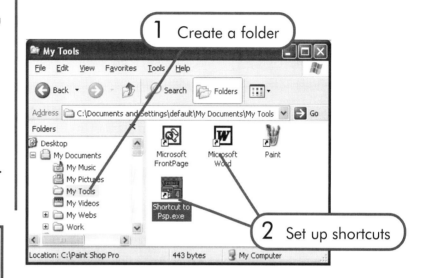

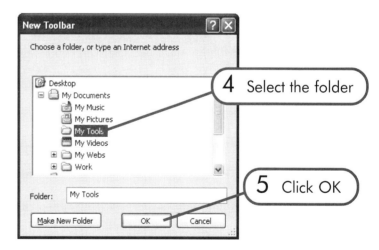

The Start menu

The Start menu can be customized in several ways. You can very easily change its appearance and control which items are shown in the main display. With just a little more effort, you can also reorganise shortcuts in the **All Programs** area, adding, moving or removing them as required.

The most dramatic change you can make is to switch to the Classic Start menu. This could be a good move if you have used and are comfortable with an earlier version of Windows. Combine this with a Windows Classic screen display to get a PC which looks very similar to one running Windows 98.

Take note

If you are one of several users on a PC, remember that every user has their own Start menu, so feel free to customise yours to suit yourself.

Select the menu style here

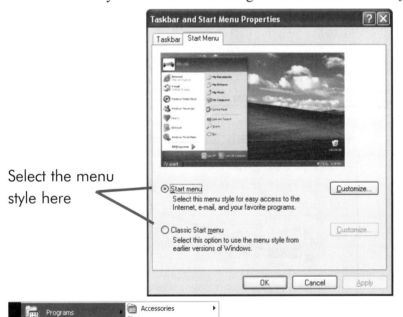

The Classic Start menu is neater, but lacks the quick links to your main applications. It can be customised in the same way as in earlier versions of Windows, with routines for adding and removing menu items.

Customizing the Start menu

1 On the Start menu tab, click Customize…

2 At the Customize Start Menu dialog box, select the icon size.

3 In the Programs area set how many shortcuts to have in the quick access set on the left – you may want more or less.

4 Select the programs to run from the Internet and the E-mail shortcuts, or turn them off if not wanted.

5 On the Advanced tab work through the Start menu items list, deciding which of the standard shortcuts to display on the right side of the menu.

6 Click ☐ OK ☐.

If you don't use the recent document list, you can remove the shortcut

The Customize options govern the content and layout of the initial Start menu display.

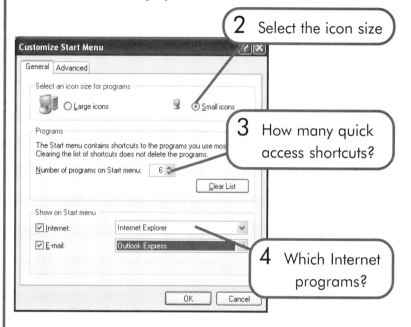

2 Select the icon size

3 How many quick access shortcuts?

4 Which Internet programs?

Highlighting can help you to locate newly installed programs

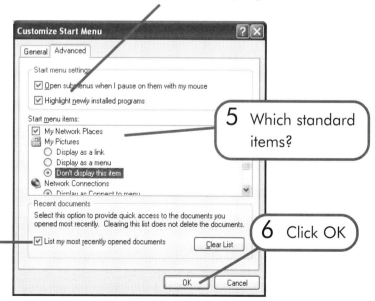

5 Which standard items?

6 Click OK

Organising the menu

Over time, as you install more applications, you may find that your **All Programs** menu becomes overcrowded. To make it more manageable, you can create group folders and move the shortcuts and folders of related applications into these. A short main menu that leads to two levels of submenus is easier to work with than one huge menu!

1 Open the Start menu, right-click on All Progams and select Open from the short menu.

2 When the Start menu folder opens, click Folders to display the Folder list – it will make it easier to see what you are doing.

3 Reorganise the menu system, using the normal file management techniques for moving, deleting and renaming files (shortcuts) and folders (submenus).

4 Click ☒ when you have done.

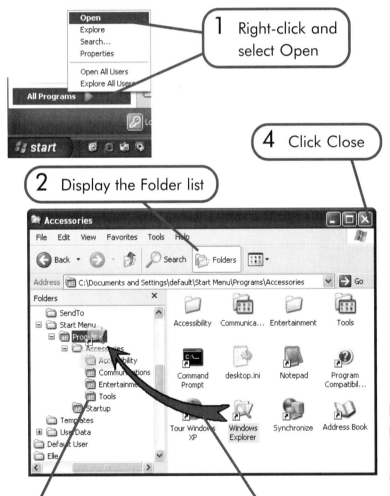

1 Right-click and select Open

2 Display the Folder list

4 Click Close

Use File > New > Folder to create a new folder (submenu)

4 Reorganise the shortcuts

Here Windows Explorer is being moved to the main Programs menu to make this useful program easier to start

Basic steps

1 Right-click on the Taskbar to open its context menu.

2 Select Adjust Date/ Time.

3 Pick the Month from the drop-down list.

4 Click on the Day.

5 Click on Hour, Minute or Second to select then either adjust with the arrows or type the correct value.

6 If you need to change the time zone, go to the Time zone tab, and select one from the drop-down list.

7 Click ⸢ Apply ⸥ to re-start the clock.

Setting the Clock

We can't leave the Taskbar without having a look at adjusting the Date and Time. This should not need doing often – PCs keep good time, and Windows even puts the clock forward and back for Summer Time!

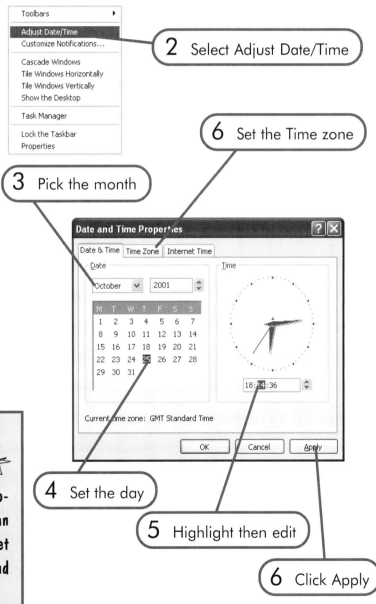

2 Select Adjust Date/Time

6 Set the Time zone

3 Pick the month

4 Set the day

5 Highlight then edit

6 Click Apply

Take note

If you want the clock to be automatically synchronized with an Internet clock, go to the Internet Time tab, turn the option on and select the service.

Summary

❏ The Taskbar can be hidden off screen or allowed to lie behind active windows, but is easiest to use if it is visible and always on top.

❏ The Taskbar can be moved to any edge of the screen, and resized if needed.

❏ Toolbars on the Taskbar offer you another way to start programs. You can create your own Toolbars.

❏ The Start menu can be switched to the Classic style if you are used to working with earlier Windows.

❏ The Start menu and its submenus are folder, and shortcuts are files. The menu can be reorganised by moving entries to new or other existing folders.

❏ The Clock can be adjusted through the Date/Time Properties dialog box.

7 The Control Panel

The settings 90

Appearance and Themes 92

Adjusting the mouse 97

Sounds 99

Regional options 100

Accessibility 102

Fonts 104

Summary 106

The settings

The **Control Panel** leads to a set of dialog boxes where you can customise many of the features of Windows to your own need and tastes.

Some settings are best left at the defaults defined by Windows; some should be set when new hardware or software is added to the system; some should be set once then left alone; a few can be fiddled with whenever you feel like a change.

You have a choice of two views:

● Category View is task oriented. You pick the category, then the task you want to perform, and the system will open the appropriate dialog box.

● Classic View lets you get directly to the dialog boxes.

You will probably find it simplest to work through the (default) Category View at first, but switch to Classic View later, once you know where to go to adjust settings.

Basic steps

1 Click then select Control Panel.

❑ Category View

2 Select a category, then at the next stage, pick a task.

❑ Classic View

3 Click Switch to Classic View.

4 Click (or double-click) an icon to open its dialog box and change its settings.

Take note

The settings which relate to the display and your interaction with the system are dealt with in this section. Others are covered elsewhere:

for **Date/Time** see page 87;

for **Printers** see Chapter 8;

for **User Accounts** and **Network Connections**, see Chapter 10;

for **Internet Connections**, see Chapter 12;

for **Add or Remove Programs** and **Performance and Maintenance**, see Chapter 9.

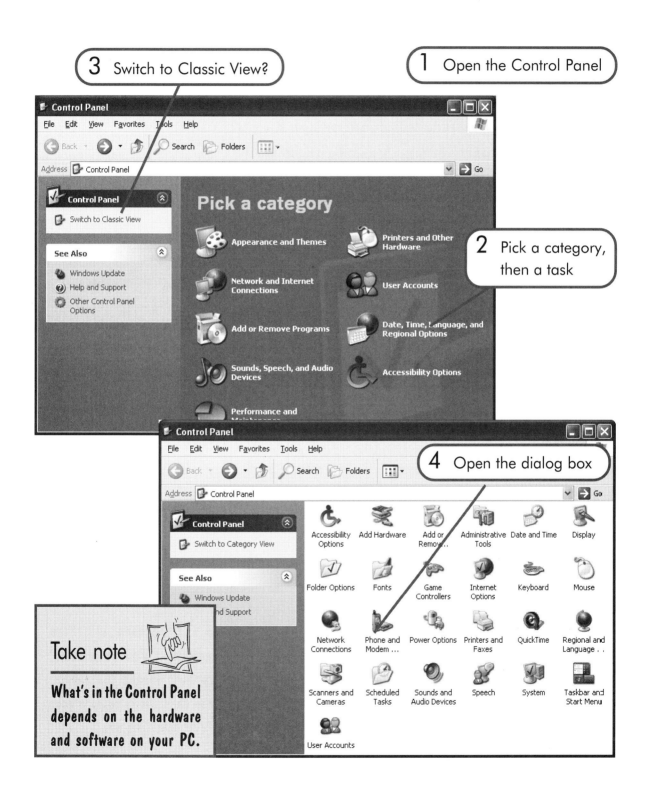

3 Switch to Classic View?

1 Open the Control Panel

2 Pick a category, then a task

4 Open the dialog box

Take note

What's in the Control Panel depends on the hardware and software on your PC.

Appearance and Themes

The settings in this category are all found on various tabs of the Display dialog box.

Display

Display options may seem to be pure frills and fancies, but they do have a serious purpose. If you spend a lot of time in front of your screen, being able to see it clearly and use it comfortably is important.

Themes

A theme sets the overall style for the Desktop – its background image, the icons for the standard Windows tools, the colours and fonts, and the sounds that are triggered by alerts and prompts. If there are parts of the theme that you don't like, you can modify them on the other tabs.

2 Open the Themes tab

Display Properties

Themes | Desktop | Screen Saver | Appearance | Settings

A theme is a background plus a set of sounds, icons, and other element to help you personalize your computer with one click.

3 Pick a theme

Theme:

Underwater (high color)   Save As...   Delete

Sample:

Active Window

Normal   Disabled   Selected

Window Text

OK   Cancel   Apply

4 Click Apply

Basic steps

1 Start from Appearance and Themes and select Change the computer's theme.

Or

2 Click the Display icon and open the Themes tab.

3 Open the Themes drop-down list, and select a theme. It will be previewed in the Sample pane.

4 When you find one you like, click Apply to fix it before you go to the other tabs to modify aspects of it.

Tip

If you modify a theme, click Save As and save it with a new name. If you ever change the theme, you can then easily restore your carefully modified one.

Same screen – different themes. Themes have an impact on every part of the display.

Desktop

The **Background** can be a single large picture, a smaller one 'tiled' to fill the screen, or a plain colour. Windows comes with a good range large and small images or you can use any graphic (preferably BMP or JPG) of your own.

With a large image, set the **Position** to *Centre* or *Stretch*; with small images, use *Tile* to fill the screen.

For a single colour desktop, set the **Background**, to *None* and pick a **Color**.

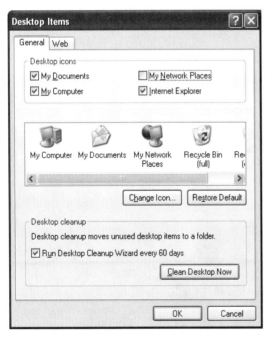

Customizing the Desktop

Click the **Customize Desktop** button to open the **Desktop Items** dialog box.

On the **General** tab you can toggle the display of the My Documents, My Computer, My Network Places and Internet Explorer icons. Turn off those that you do not use. You can also select new images for the standard icons, and run the Desktop Cleanup Wizard – either at that time or set it to run regularly. (See page 76 for more on this Wizard.)

On the **Web** tab, you can link to a Web page to make that the background image. I suspect that this is probably only likely to be of interest to people who have permanently open lines to the Web and who need up-to-the-minute information from a specialist service.

Appearance

This controls the Windows and buttons styles, colour schemes and the size of fonts.

Start by choosing the Windows and buttons style. Classic Style gives you a much wider range of colour schemes, including several high contrast schemes for the visually impaired.

You should also select **Large** and **Extra large Fonts** if easy viewing is needed.

Whichever scheme you choose, you can modify it through the **Effects** and **Advanced** options.

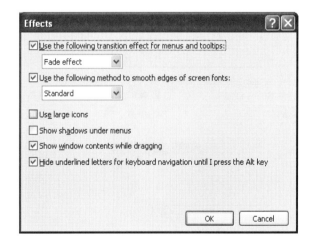

The **Effects** have minimal impact, but play with them to see which you like.

In the **Advanced** dialog box you can adjust the size, colour and font of individual elements.

To modify an item, click on it in the preview pane, or select it from the Item drop-down list, then set its size, colour, and font attributes as required.

When you have finished, click **OK** to return to the **Properties** panel.

Screen Savers

These are fun but serve little real purpose nowadays. (On an old monitor, if a static image was left on too long, it could burn into the screen.) A screen saver switches to a moving image after the system has been left inactive for a few minutes. **Preview** the ones that are on offer. **Settings** allows you to adjust the images.

If you turn on the option **On resume, password protect** (or **display Welcome screen**, where there are several users), then once the saver has started, your password will have to be entered before the screen – and your work – is visible again.

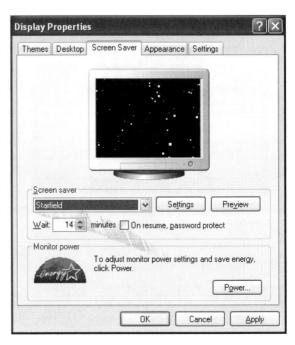

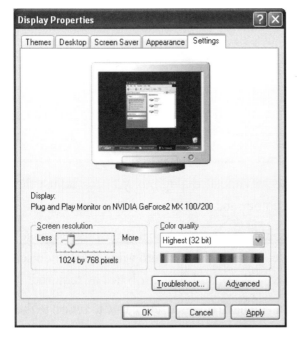

Settings

Play with the other panels as much as you like, but treat this one with respect. In particular, leave the **Advanced** options alone unless you are unhappy with the current display *and* know what you are doing. You can switch to a display mode that is not properly supported by your hardware, resulting in a screen which is difficult or impossible to read – and therefore to correct!

If you do produce an unreadable screen, reboot the system using the Startup disk – you did make one, didn't you – and restore the default setting from there.

Mouse

Adjusting the mouse

❑ Buttons tab

1 Set the Double-click speed.

2 Double-click in the Test area to see if the system responds.

❑ Pointer Options tab

3 Set the Motion speed.

4 Turn on any Visibility options that you might find useful.

Start from the **Mouse** icon in **Printers and other hardware**.

Don't **Switch primary and secondary buttons** (so the left and right buttons do each other's job) unless you are left-handed and only ever use the one PC. You will only confuse yourself.

The **Double-Click Speed** determines the difference between a proper double-click and two separate clicks.

On the **Pointer Options** tab, set the **Motion**. Speed is linked to distance, so that the faster you move the mouse, the further the pointer goes.

For better **Visibility** on an LCD screen, turn on **Pointer Trails**.

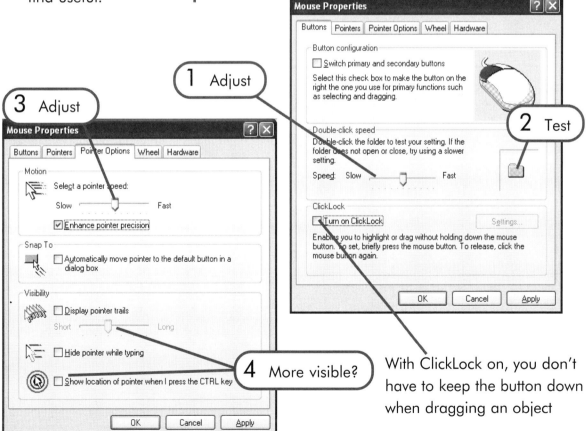

With ClickLock on, you don't have to keep the button down when dragging an object

Pointers

There are alternative Schemes, including ones with large and extra large pointers. You can also pick your own images (and animated ones from any Desktop themes you have installed) to link to chosen mouse actions.

Basic steps

❑ Pointers tab

1 Pick a Scheme.

2 Select an action.

3 Click [Browse...].

4 Pick a cursor image for the action.

5 Click [Open].

❑ Repeat Steps 2 to 5 for any other actions.

6 Click [OK].

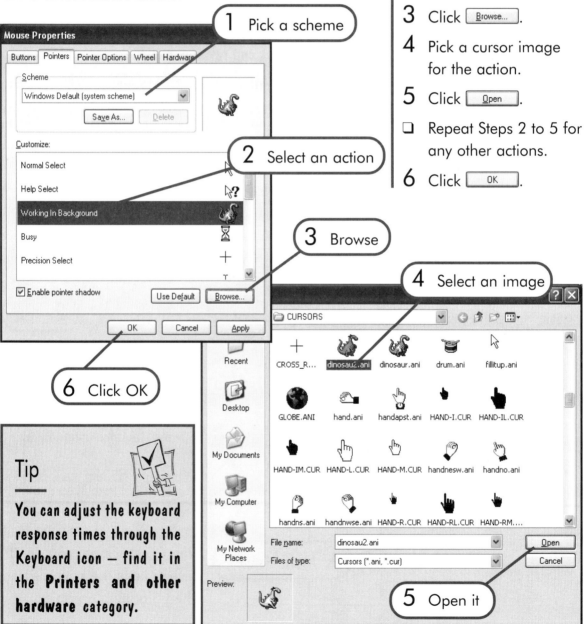

1 Pick a scheme

2 Select an action

3 Browse

4 Select an image

6 Click OK

5 Open it

Tip

You can adjust the keyboard response times through the Keyboard icon — find it in the **Printers and other hardware** category.

Basic steps

Sounds and
Audio Devices

1 Start from the Sounds, Speech and Audio devices category of the Control Panel and when the dialog box opens go to the Sounds tab.

2 Pick a Scheme.

3 Select an event.

4 Click ▶ to preview its sound.

5 Sample a few more and go back to Step 2 and try alternative schemes until you find one you prefer.

6 To set individual sounds, select the event then pick a new sound from the Sounds list or Browse for an alternative.

7 Click ⎡ Apply ⎤ or ⎡ OK ⎤.

Sounds

Windows allows you to attach sounds to events. These can be seen as useful ways of alerting you to what's happening or as more modern noise pollution. It all depends upon your point of view. I like a fanfare when the system is ready to start work (to wake me up – well, you wait so long!) but few other sounds. Try them out – the Utopia sounds are worth listening to.

The other tabs can be used to change the Audio and Voice devices or fine-tune their volume controls. The devices are best left to the system. The volume controls can be reached more simply from the 🔊 icon on the Taskbar.

Controls the speaker settings

Use the Test hardware and Troubleshoot routines on these tabs if you have problems, otherwise, leave these tabs alone

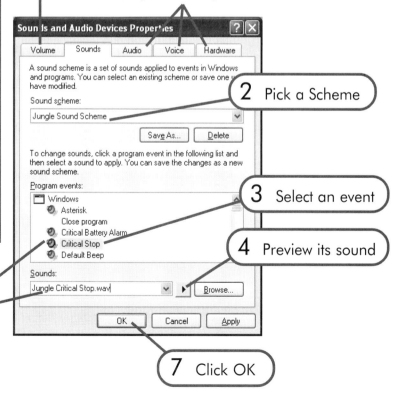

2 Pick a Scheme

3 Select an event

4 Preview its sound

6 Select a new sound for an event?

7 Click OK

Regional options

Regional and
Language ...

The **Regional and Language Options** control the units of measurement and the styles used by applications for displaying dates, time, currency and other numbers. The choice of region sets the basic formats, but any or all of these can be customized.

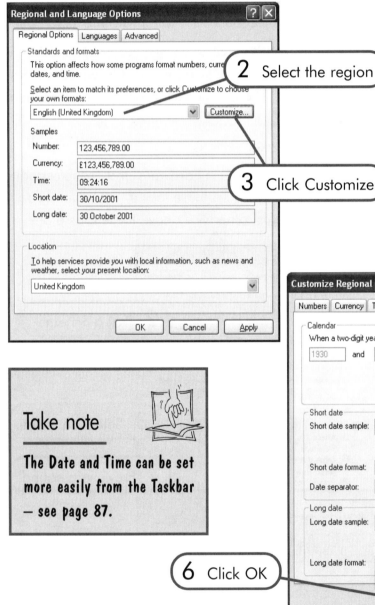

2 Select the region

3 Click Customize

1 Start from Date, Time, Language and Regional Options of the Control Panel and click Regional and Language Options.

2 Select the region.

❑ Customizing

3 Click [Customize...].

4 Open the tab.

5 To change any aspect, pick from its drop-down list.

6 Click [OK].

4 Open a tab

5 Pick a format option

6 Click OK

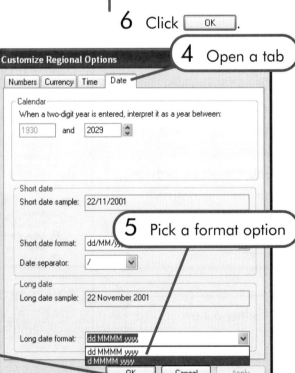

Take note

The Date and Time can be set more easily from the Taskbar – see page 87.

100

Basic steps

1 Switch to the Languages tab.

2 Click ⟨ Details... ⟩.

3 At the Text Services and Input Languages box, click Add and pick the language.

4 To define a shortcut for switching the keyboard, click ⟨ Key Settings... ⟩.

5 Click ⟨ OK ⟩.

Add other languages

Use this link if you want to be able to enter text using the keyboard for another language. This changes the letters produced by the keys and is best suited to touch-typists who are used to a foreign keyboard. Most of us are better off selecting foreign characters from the Character Map (see page 151).

● You can switch between keyboards using the Language bar on Taskbar. If you prefer, you can also define a keyboard shortcut.

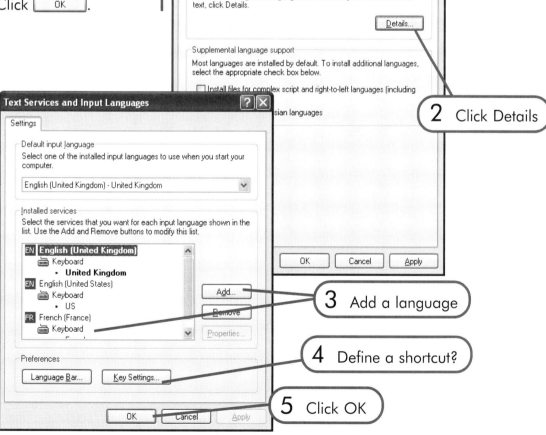

1 Go to Languages

2 Click Details

3 Add a language

4 Define a shortcut?

5 Click OK

Accessibility

Accessibility
Options

These offer a range of ways to make life easier for people with sight, hearing or motor control disabilities – though the keyboard alternative to the mouse may well be useful to other people as well.

Keyboard

With **StickyKeys** you can type [Ctrl], [Shift] and [Alt] combinations by pressing one key at a time, rather than all at once.

FilterKeys solves the problem of repetition of keystrokes caused by slow typing.

ToggleKeys play sounds when any of the Lock keys are pressed.

Sound

These replace sound warnings with visible alerts.

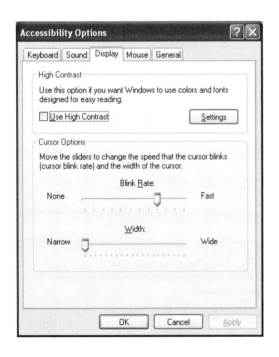

Display

The High Contrast displays can be selected from here, as well as from the Display panel. If you click the [Settings] button, you can set up a keyboard shortcut to toggle between High Contrast and normal displays – useful if there are times when you need a much more visible display.

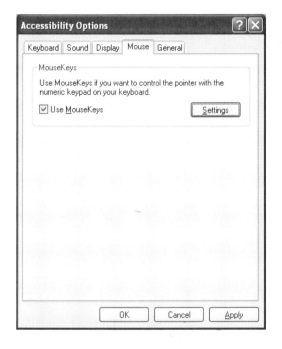

Mouse

With this turned on, the arrow keys on the Number pad can be used to move the mouse, and the central [5] acts as the left mouse button. It is more limited than the mouse – you can only move up, down, left or right and not diagonally – but it is easier to control.

Click the **Settings…** button to open the Settings for MouseKeys dialog box, where you can experiment to find the most workable levels.

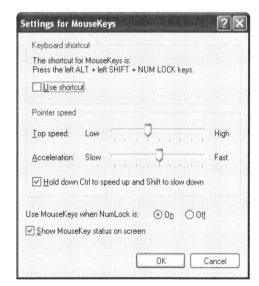

General

If you are using any of the Accessibility options, check this panel to make sure that they are turning on and off as and when you want them.

This illustration shows the standard High Contrast display setting. If required, larger fonts could be set for the panel and button text.

Fonts

Fonts

There is one school of thought that says you can never have enough fonts. There is a decent core supplied with Windows itself, and you will normally acquire more with any word-processor and desktop publishing packages that you install. If these are not enough for you, there are whole disks full of fonts available commercially and through the shareware distributors.

Installing new fonts is quick and easy.

Basic steps

❑ Adding fonts

1 Place the disk of new fonts into a drive.

2 Open the File menu and select Install New Font…

3 Select the drive and folder and wait while the system reads the names of the fonts on the disk.

4 Click [Select All], or work through the list and select the ones you want to install.

5 Click [OK].

2 Use File > Install New Font

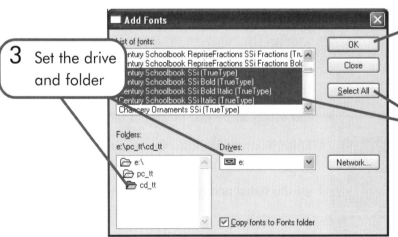

5 Click OK

3 Set the drive and folder

4 Select All or some

Basic steps

Removing unwanted fonts

1 Click [AB] the Similarity tool.

2 Pick a font to list by, then select and Open it from its context menu.

3 Select and Open any *Very similar* font.

4 Click [Done] to close the viewer.

5 If it is not useful, press [Delete] to remove it.

This will save space on the hard disk, speed up Windows' Start Up and produce a shorter set to hunt through when you are setting a font in an application. Listing fonts by similarity helps to identify unnecessary ones.

(2 Open a base font)

(1 List by Similarity)

(4 Click Done)

(3 Open a Very similar font)

There can be subtle differences between the screen and printed appearance of a font – print a sample for a closer look.

Summary

❑ The Control Panel contains routines that determine the settings of some of the most basic features of how Windows works.

❑ You can display the Control Panel in Category or Classic view.

❑ The Display give you plenty of scope for personal preferences. Set the background, patterns, colour scheme and fonts to suit yourself – but don't change the Advanced Settings unless you have to.

❑ Adjust the mouse and keyboard responses to your own needs at an early stage, then leave them alone.

❑ There are several mouse pointer schemes, and individual pointers can be redesigned.

❑ Sounds can be assigned to events, to alert you when things happen.

❑ The Regional settings control the appearance of dates, times, currency and numbers in most Windows Applications.

❑ Windows has a number of Accessibility Options to make the screen easier to read and the mouse and keyboard easier to control.

❑ New Fonts can be installed easily. It is just as easy to examine fonts and to remove unnecessary ones.

8 Printers

Printer settings 108

Adding a printer 110

Managing the queue 112

Direct printing 113

Summary 114

Printer settings

Windows XP knows about printers, just as it knows about most other bits of hardware that you might attach to your system. Check your printer the settings now. Make sure that they are how you would *normally* want to use it – the settings can be changed for any special print job, using the Print Setup routine of any application program.

Basic steps

1 Click ⟪ *start* ⟫.

2 Select Printers and Faxes.

3 Right-click a printer to open its short menu and select Properties.

Or

4 Select Set printer properties from the Tasks list.

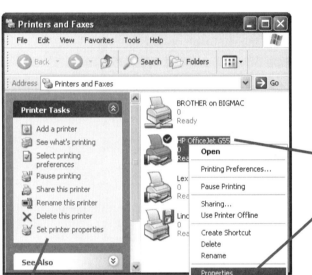

3 Right-click and select Properties

4 Click Set printer properties

All printers have a General tab, showing a summary of the key features and settings. If you are on a network, there will be a Sharing tab where you can control other users' access to your printer.

The main options are set on the Advanced tab and in the Printing Preferences panel (reached through the button on this tab).

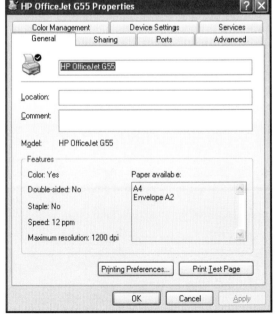

On the Advanced tab, check that the printer is set for the right paper size. To change a size, click on it – a drop-down list will appear from which you can pick the correct size.

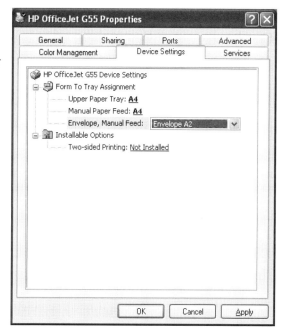

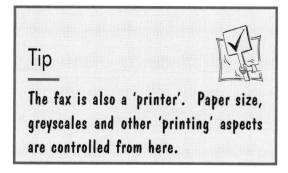

Tip

The fax is also a 'printer'. Paper size, greyscales and other 'printing' aspects are controlled from here.

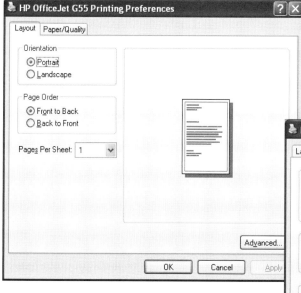

In the Printing Preferences dialog box, select the default Layout (above) and Paper/Quality options (right).

Adding a printer

If your printer is not detected and installed automatically by the plug and play technology, you can add it yourself easily. There is a wizard to take you through the steps, and Windows XP has *drivers* for almost all printers made up to mid-2001. (Drivers convert the formatting information from an application into the right codes for the printer.) If you have a *very* new machine, use the drivers on the printer's setup disk.

1 Click Add a printer

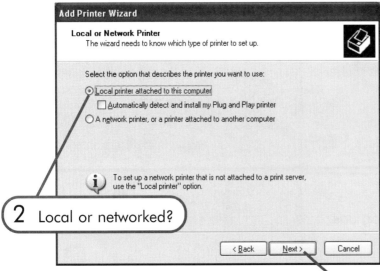

2 Local or networked?

Click Next after completing each step

1 Click Add a printer in the Print Tasks set to start the wizard.

2 If you are on a net-work, select Local (attached to your PC) or Network printer.

3 Select the Port – nor-mally LPT1.

Either

4 Pick the Manufacturer then the Printer from the lists.

or

5 Insert a disk with the printer driver and click Have Disk...

6 Change the name if you like – a networked printer should have clear recognisable name to identify it.

7 Set the printer as the default if appropriate.

8 At the final stage opt for the test print, then click Finish and wait.

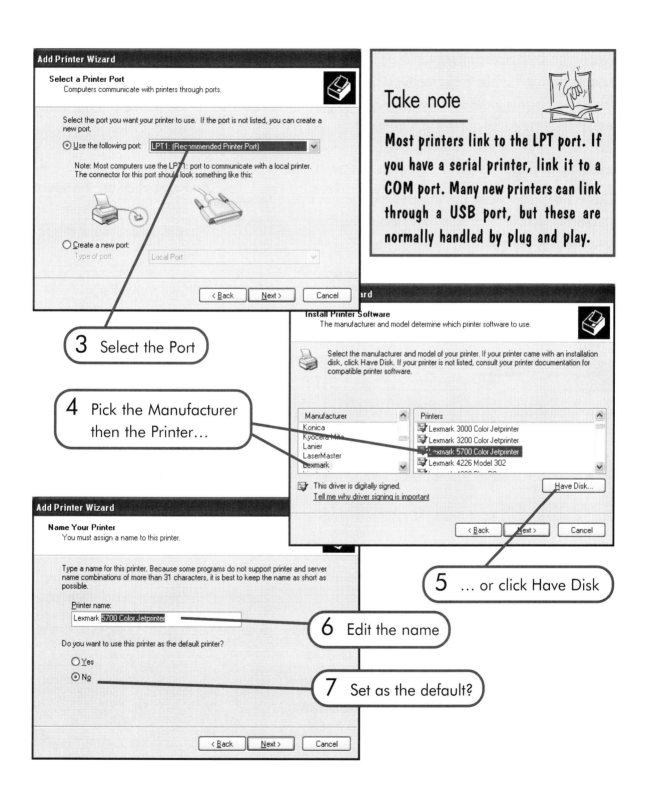

Add Printer Wizard

Select a Printer Port
Computers communicate with printers through ports.

Select the port you want your printer to use. If the port is not listed, you can create a new port.

⊙ Use the following port: LPT1: (Recommended Printer Port)

Note: Most computers use the LPT1: port to communicate with a local printer. The connector for this port should look something like this:

○ Create a new port:
Type of port: Local Port

< Back   Next >   Cancel

Take note

Most printers link to the LPT port. If you have a serial printer, link it to a COM port. Many new printers can link through a USB port, but these are normally handled by plug and play.

Install Printer Software
The manufacturer and model determine which printer software to use.

Select the manufacturer and model of your printer. If your printer came with an installation disk, click Have Disk. If your printer is not listed, consult your printer documentation for compatible printer software.

Manufacturer	Printers
Konica	Lexmark 3000 Color Jetprinter
Kyocera Mita	Lexmark 3200 Color Jetprinter
Lanier	Lexmark 5700 Color Jetprinter
LaserMaster	Lexmark 4226 Model 302
Lexmark	

This driver is digitally signed.
Tell me why driver signing is important

Have Disk...

< Back   Next >   Cancel

3 Select the Port

4 Pick the Manufacturer then the Printer…

Add Printer Wizard

Name Your Printer
You must assign a name to this printer.

Type a name for this printer. Because some programs do not support printer and server name combinations of more than 31 characters, it is best to keep the name as short as possible.

Printer name:
Lexmark 5700 Color Jetprinter

Do you want to use this printer as the default printer?

○ Yes
⊙ No

5 … or click Have Disk

6 Edit the name

7 Set as the default?

< Back   Next >   Cancel

Managing the queue

When you send a document for printing, Windows XP will happily handle it in the background. It prepares the file for the printer, stores it in a queue if the printer is already busy or off-line, pushes the pages out one at a time and deletes the temporary files it has created. Nothing visible happens on screen – unless the printer runs out of paper or has other faults.

This is fine when things run smoothly. However, if you decide you want to cancel the printing of a document, then you do need to see things. No problem!

1 Open the Printers folder, right-click on the active printer and select Open.

Or

2 Right-click on the 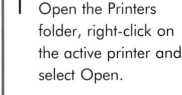 icon in the Taskbar and select the printer.

❑ To cancel printing

3 Select the file(s).

4 Press [Delete] or open the Document menu and select Cancel.

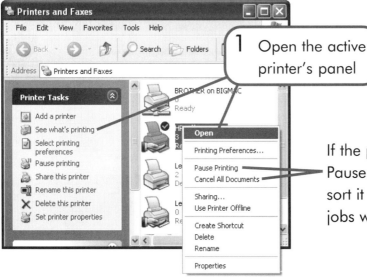

1 Open the active printer's panel

If the printer's playing up use Pause Printing to give you time to sort it out, or stop all pending print jobs with Cancel All Documents

3 Select the file

4 Use Document > Cancel

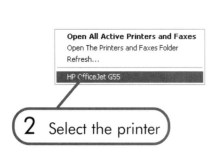

2 Select the printer

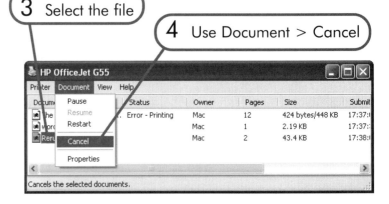

Direct printing

1 Run My Computer or Windows Explorer and locate the document file to be printed.

2 Select the file.

3 Click Print this file in the Tasks list.

❑ Windows will open the related application, print from there then close the application.

You do not necessarily have to load a document into an application to print it. Windows XP can print many types of documents directly from the files.

Bitmapped graphics (.BMP files), plain text and the documents from any Microsoft Office application can be printed in this way, as can those from other newer software.

1 Run My Computer

3 Click Print this file

2 Locate the file

Tip

You can also print a file by right-clicking on it and selecting **Print** from the context menu.

Summary

❑ Printer settings can be adjusted if wanted. The Paper and layout options should be checked.

❑ Adding a new printer is easy. Windows has drivers for almost all printers, though you may need a manufacturer's disk with very new models.

❑ Printing is handled in the background, so that – apart from slowing things up a bit – it does not interfere with your other work.

❑ Files are stored in a queue before printing. You can change their order or delete them if necessary.

❑ You can print a file from My Computer by selecting Print from the file's context menu or using the Print this file task.

9 Disk housekeeping

The System Tools 116

Error-checking 118

Disk Defragmenter 119

Backup 120

Disk Cleanup 123

Add/Remove Programs 124

System Restore 126

Formatting a floppy 128

Caring for floppies 129

Summary 130

The System Tools

These programs will help to keep your disks in good condition, and your data safe.

Backup – enables you to keep safe copies of your important files, and to recover lost data.

Disk Cleanup – finds and removes unused files;

Disk Defragmenter – optimises the organisation of storage to maximize the disk's speed and efficiency;

Error-check – finds and fixes errors in data stored on disks;

Scheduled Tasks – lets you perform maintenance at set times;

System Information – gives (technical) information about what's going on inside your computer;

System Restore – backs up essential files, so that the system can be restored to normal after a crash.

Most of the tools can be started from the **System Tools** part of the Start menu; some are reached through the hard disk's Properties panel.

Basic steps

1 Click **start**.
2 Point to All Programs
3 Point to Accessories.
4 Point to System Tools.
5 Click to select a tool.

Character Map and Clipboard Viewer are accessories, not tools – I don't know why Windows puts them on this menu.

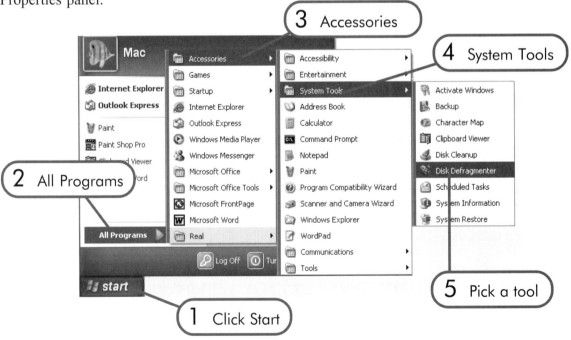

3 Accessories

4 System Tools

2 All Programs

5 Pick a tool

1 Click Start

116

Basic steps

1 Open My Computer, right-click on the drive for the context menu.

2 Select Properties.

3 Click [Disk Cleanup].

Or

4 Go to the Tools tab to start the Error-check, Defragmenter or Backup.

Routine chores

The four system tools that are needed for the routine housekeeping can also be reached from the Properties box of any disk. The messages will remind you of chores you have been neglecting!

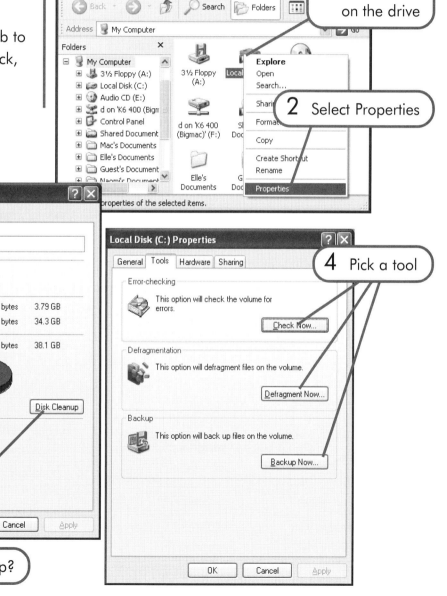

Error-checking

Data is stored on disks in *allocation units*. A small file may fit on a single unit, but others are spread over many. A file's units may be in a continuous run or scattered over the disk (see *Disk Defragmenter,* opposite), but they are all kept together by links from one to the next. Sometimes the links get corrupted leaving *Lost fragments*, with no known links to any file, or *Cross-linked files*, where two are chained to the same unit of data.

The magnetic surface of the disk may also (rarely) become corrupted, creating *Bad sectors* where data cannot be stored.

The Error-checking routine can identify these and, with a bit of luck, retrieve any data written there and transfer it to a safe part of the disk. It is very simple to run, with only two options at the start, and nothing for you to do once it's running.

● With **Automatically fix file system errors** on, it will try to solve any problems that it meets – and it will do this better than you or I could, so leave it to it!

● **Scan for and attempt recovery of bad sectors** will test the surface of the disk, to make sure that files can be stored safely, and rebuild it if necessary. This automatically runs the first option.

If no option is set, the routine simply checks that the files are stored safely.

1 Go to the Tools tab of the disk's Properties dialog box (page 117) and click  Check Now... .

2 For a quick check, turn off the options.

3 If you think the disk has errors, turn on one or other option.

4 Click Start .

Take note

Once the error-checker starts work, you can't do anything at all on the PC. A quick check only takes a few moments; a full check can take an hour or more.

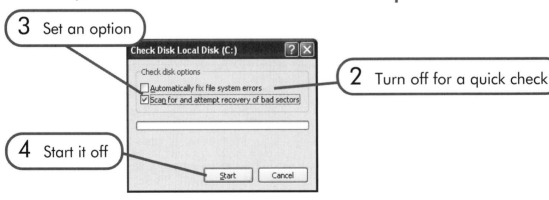

3 Set an option

2 Turn off for a quick check

4 Start it off

Check Disk Local Disk (C:)
Check disk options
☐ Automatically fix file system errors
☑ Scan for and attempt recovery of bad sectors

Start   Cancel

Basic steps

1 Run the Disk Defragmenter from the Start menu or the disk's Properties box.

2 Click and wait while it analyses the disk.

3 If the report recommends defragmenting, click `Defragment`.

When you first start to write data onto a disk, the files are stored one after the other, with each occupying a continuous run of disk space. When you access one of these files, the drive simply finds the start point, then reads the data in a single sweep.

After the disk has been in use for some time, holes begin to appear in the layout, and not all files are stored in a continuous area. Some have been deleted, others will have grown during editing, so that they no longer fit in their original slot, but now have parts stored elsewhere on the disk. When you store a new file, there may not be a single space large enough for it, and it is stored in scattered sections. The drive is becoming *fragmented*. The data is still safe, but the access speed will suffer as the drive now has to hunt for each fragment of the file.

Disk Defragmenter should be run from time to time to pull scattered files together, so that they are stored in continuous blocks.

Take note

Defragmenting a disk is not a quick job. It can take well over an hour to reorganise the files on a hard disk and you shouldn't use the PC during this time.

A disk can be divided into several volumes, but normally *volume* means the C: drive

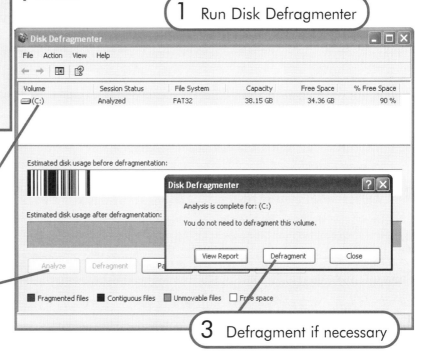

1 Run Disk Defragmenter

2 Click Analyze

3 Defragment if necessary

Backup

If program files are accidentally deleted, it is a nuisance but not a major problem as you can reinstall the application from the original disks. Data files are different. How much is your data worth to you? How long would it take you to rewrite that report or reedit that image? Individual files can be copied onto floppies for safekeeping, but if you have more than one or two it is simpler to use Backup. A backup job is easily set up and will more than pay for itself in time and effort if you ever need it!

Backups can be done on floppy disks. This is fine for home use or in a small business where there's not a lot to backup – with compression, over 2Mb of data will fit on one disk. If you intend to backup large quantities of data regularly, invest £100 or so in a tape drive so you don't have to struggle with a pile of floppies.

Advanced Backup settings

These can be set through the **Advanced** button on the summary panel. The main option is the *Type of Backup*:

- **Normal**, copies all the selected files and marks them as backed up;

- **Copy**, copies all the selected files, but without marking them as backed up;

- **Incremental** saves only those changed since last the Normal backup;

- **Differential** also saves only changed files, but without marking them as backed up;

- **Daily** saves only files created on the current day.

You can also specify the nature, placing and – most usefully – *scheduling*. If you are using a backup tape or other high capacity media, it makes sense to run the backup at non-working times.

1 Click Backup Now on the disk's Properties dialog box. You can back up or restore files. Select backup.

2 If you want to backup everything on your hard drives – select All information on this computer.

3 If you opt to back up selected files, you will see an Explorer-style display. Click the ⊞ icons to open out the folders as necessary.

❑ Tick a folder to back up everything in it.

❑ To select items within a folder, click on its name to open it, then tick individual items.

4 Select the medium (tape, disk, etc) and the drive.

5 Give the backup job a name which describes the file selection and/ or the date.

6 At the final stage, you will see a summary of the backup settings. If everything is OK, click Finish. If you are backing up a lot of data on to floppies, be ready to change the disks on request.

Backup or Restore Wizard

Items to Back Up
You can back up any combination of drives, folders, or files.

Double-click an item on the left to see its contents on the right. Then select the check box next to any drive, folder, or file that you want to back up.

Items to back up:

- My Pictures
- My Tools
- My Videos
- My Webs
- Work
  - Accounts
    - 2000
    - 2001
  - Database

Name	Type
charts.xls	Microsoft Ex...
sysupsum.xls	Microsoft Ex...

3 Select the items to back up

< Back   Next >   Cancel

Select single files
Select entire folders

Backup or Restore Wizard

Backup Type, Destination, and Name
Your files and settings are stored in the destination you specify.

Select the backup type:

File

Choose a place to save your backup:

3½ Floppy (A:)   Browse...

4 Select the medium

Type a name for this backup:

26Nov

5 Give it a name

Set the type, schedule or other options

< Back

Backup or Restore Wizard

Completing the Backup or Restore Wizard

You have created the following backup settings:

Name: A:\26Nov.bkf

Description: Set created 02/11/2001 at 17:08

Contents: My documents and settings

Location: File

To close this wizard and start the backup, click Finish.

To specify additional backup options, click Advanced.   Advanced...

< Back   Finish   Cancel

6 Check and click Finish

Tip

You must use removable media so that you can store the backup elsewhere — in a fireproof safe or another building for best security.

Restoring files

With any luck this will never be necessary! But it's not difficult to do in any case. All you need to do is select the files that you want to restore, and let the wizard get on with it!

1 Run Backup, and select Restore at the opening panel.

2 Insert the disk or tape with the backup into its drive.

3 Click Browse and select the backup file.

4 Open the folders as necessary until you can see the files and folders that you want to restore.

5 Tick the files to select them.

6 Click Next – that's it.

3 Browse for the file

4 Open the folders

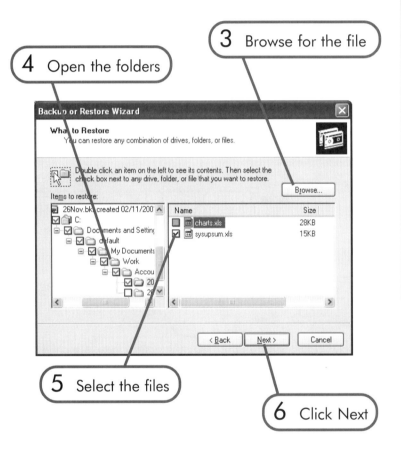

5 Select the files

6 Click Next

Basic steps

1 Run Disk Cleanup from the Start menu or click [Disk Cleanup] on the disk's Properties panel.

2 After it has checked the system, the Cleanup panel opens. Select the areas to be cleaned.

3 Click [OK].

This is a neat little utility, and well worth running regularly – especially if you spend much time on the Internet. When you are surfing, your browser stores the files for the text, graphics and programs on the Web pages that you visit. This makes sense, as it means that if you go back to a page (either in the same session or at a later date), the browser can redraw it from the files, rather than having to download the whole lot again. However, if you don't revisit sites much, you can build up a lot of unwanted clutter on your disk. You can empty this cache from within your browser, but Cleanup will also do it.

The Recycle Bin can be emptied directly, or as part of the Cleanup.

Programs often create temporary files, but do not always remove them. Cleanup will also tidy up after them.

Tip

If you really want to create some extra space on your system, check through your programs and the Windows Setup and remove any that you do not use. The More Options panel leads to the Add/ Remove Programs routine – see page 126 for more on this.

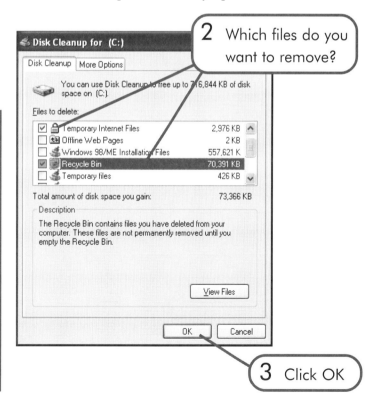

2 Which files do you want to remove?

3 Click OK

Add/Remove Programs

Add or
Remov…

Any software written to the Windows standards should be easy to install and – just as important – easy to remove. Unwanted parts of Windows XP can also be removed – and you can add accessories that were omitted during the initial installation.

1 Go to Add/Remove Programs

2 Select the program

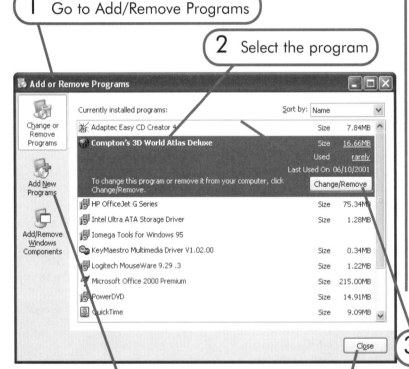

❑ Removing Programs

1 Go to the More Options tab of Disk Cleanup and click Clean up under Installed Programs.

2 Select the program.

3 Click [Change/Remove] or [Remove] – some programs have separate buttons.

❑ You may be asked to confirm the removal of files that may be used by other programs – if in doubt, keep them.

4 Click [Close].

3 Click Change/Remove

You can install from here, but it is simpler to use any new software's Setup routine

4 Click Close

Tip

You may need the original CD-ROM to uninstall some software.

Take note

If data files have been stored in the program's folder, the routine will not be able to remove them – use My Computer to tidy up any remnants.

❏ Trimming Windows

5 On the More Options tab of Disk Cleanup click Clean up under Windows components – a Wizard will run. Wait while it checks your system.

6 To remove an entire set of components, click on the checkbox to clear it.

7 To remove individual files, select the set and click [Details...].

8 Clear the checkboxes for unwanted items then click [OK].

9 At the main panel, click [Next >] to start the removals.

Take note

To add new accessories or other features, tick the checkboxes instead of clearing them!

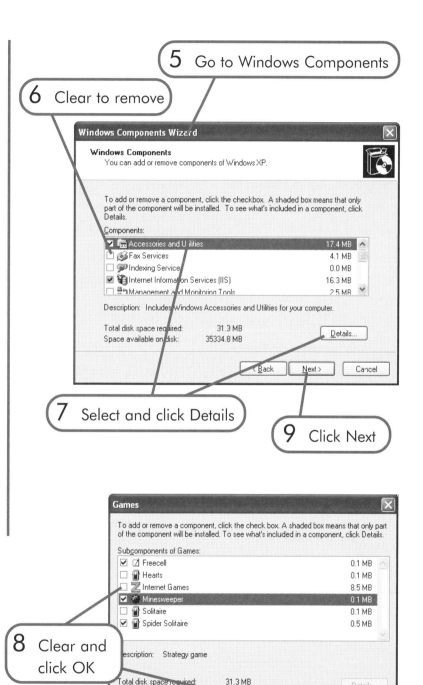

5 Go to Windows Components

6 Clear to remove

7 Select and click Details

9 Click Next

8 Clear and click OK

125

System Restore

You may never need to use this – but if you do, you will be very glad that it was there! System Restore helps you to recover from disaster. It works by taking copies of your essential files at regular intervals – once or twice a day. If any of those files become corrupted or erased – accidentally or otherwise – System Restore will put things back to how they were. Just run the application and select a restore point when things were well – normally the previous day's, but you may need to go back further if there have been problems lurking for a while.

For extra security, you can create your own 'restore points' before installing new software. A badly-designed application may occasionally mess up existing settings.

1 Run System Restore.

2 Select Restore my computer to an earlier time and click [Next >].

3 Pick a date and time and click [Next >].

4 Confirm or cancel at the final screen.

❏ Create a restore point

5 Select Create a restore point and click [Next >].

6 Enter a description and click [Next >].

1 Run System Restore

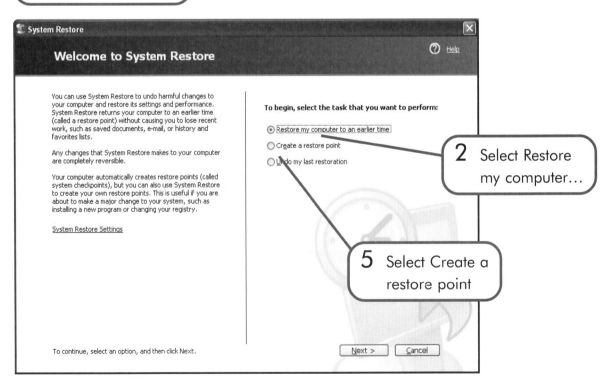

2 Select Restore my computer...

5 Select Create a restore point

126

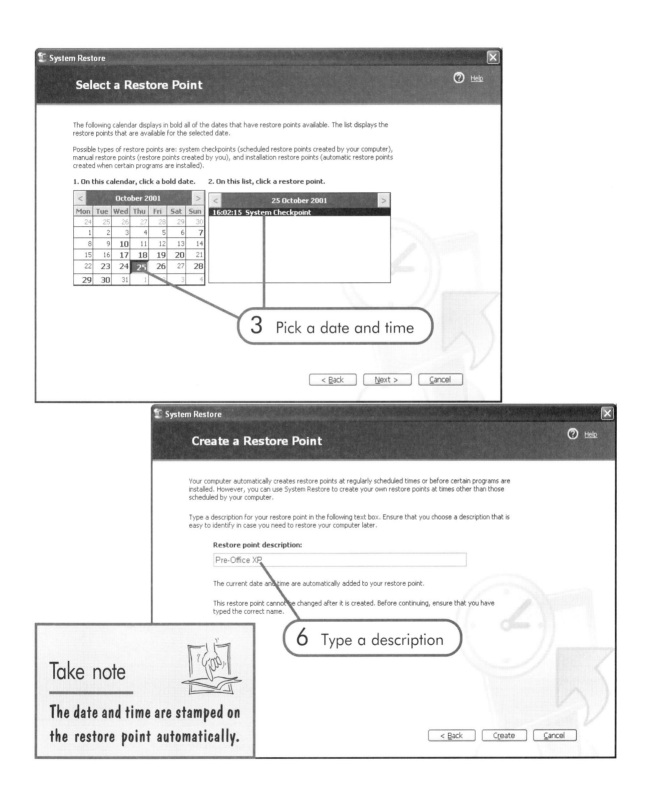

System Restore

Select a Restore Point

? Help

The following calendar displays in bold all of the dates that have restore points available. The list displays the restore points that are available for the selected date.

Possible types of restore points are: system checkpoints (scheduled restore points created by your computer), manual restore points (restore points created by you), and installation restore points (automatic restore points created when certain programs are installed).

1. On this calendar, click a bold date.   **2. On this list, click a restore point.**

<	October 2001					>
Mon	Tue	Wed	Thu	Fri	Sat	Sun
24	25	26	27	28	29	30
1	2	3	4	5	6	7
8	9	10	11	12	13	14
15	16	17	18	19	20	21
22	23	24	25	26	27	28
29	30	31	1	2	3	4

<	25 October 2001	>
16:02:15 System Checkpoint		

3 Pick a date and time

< Back   Next >   Cancel

System Restore

Create a Restore Point

? Help

Your computer automatically creates restore points at regularly scheduled times or before certain programs are installed. However, you can use System Restore to create your own restore points at times other than those scheduled by your computer.

Type a description for your restore point in the following text box. Ensure that you choose a description that is easy to identify in case you need to restore your computer later.

Restore point description:

Pre-Office XP

The current date and time are automatically added to your restore point.

This restore point cannot be changed after it is created. Before continuing, ensure that you have typed the correct name.

6 Type a description

< Back   Create   Cancel

Take note

The date and time are stamped on the restore point automatically.

127

Formatting a floppy

Before you can use a new floppy disk, it must be **formatted**. This marks out magnetic tracks on the disk surface, dividing the area up into numbered blocks to provide organised storage. The **Format** command does this job – all you have to do is make sure that you know what kind of disk you are formatting, and possibly set an option.

PC disks are almost always High-Density (HD) standard – 3.5 inch, 1.44Mb capacities. You may occasionally meet a 720Kb Double-Density (DD) 3.5 inch disk.

Most new disks are now sold pre-formatted, so a full format may rarely be needed, but **Quick Format** is very handy – use this to clear files off a floppy – it's faster than deleting them!

1 Insert the disk into the drive.

2 Run My Computer or Windows Explorer.

3 Right-click on the A: drive icon and select Format....

4 Make sure that it is set for the right Capacity.

5 Set a Format option if wanted.

6 Click [Start].

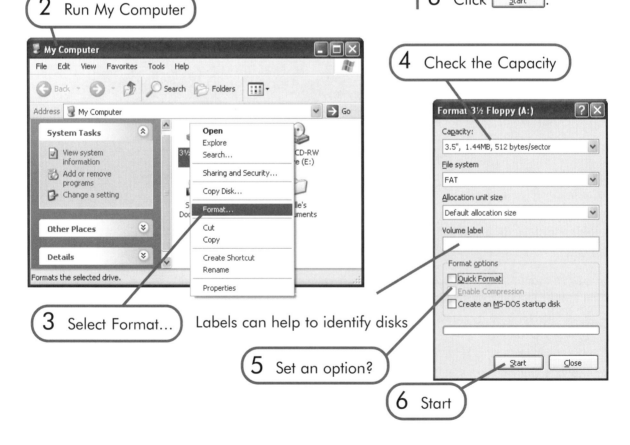

2 Run My Computer

3 Select Format...

Labels can help to identify disks

4 Check the Capacity

5 Set an option?

6 Start

Caring for floppies

❏ Disk drives can be mounted horizontally or vertically, but a disk will only go in one way round. If it won't fit, don't force it. Try it the other way round.

The modern 3.5 inch floppy is quite a tough beast. Its plastic casing protects it well against grime, knocks and splashes of coffee, but it still has enemies.

● Heat, damp and magnetism will go through the casing and corrupt the data on the disk beneath. So, keep your disks away from radiators, sunny windowsills, and magnets.

● Heavy electrical machinery and mains cables should also be avoided as they too produce magnetic fields.

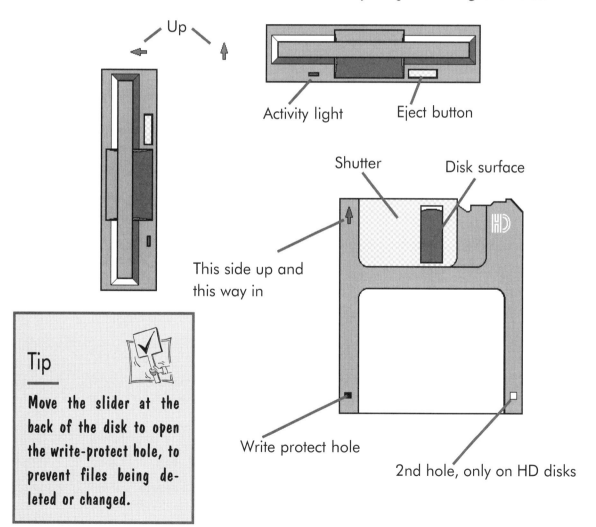

Up

Activity light   Eject button

Shutter   Disk surface

This side up and this way in

Tip

Move the slider at the back of the disk to open the write-protect hole, to prevent files being deleted or changed.

Write protect hole

2nd hole, only on HD disks

Summary

- ❏ Windows XP is supplied with a set of very useful system tools.

- ❏ The error-checker can find and fix errors on your disks.

- ❏ The Disk Defragmenter should be run regularly to ensure that files are stored compactly, and can therefore be loaded faster.

- ❏ Use Backup regularly to ensure that you have safe copies of your data files.

- ❏ Disk Cleanup offers an easy way to find and remove unwanted files.

- ❏ Use Add/Remove Programs to clear unused applications and Windows components off your hard disk.

- ❏ System Restore takes copies of essential system files so that they can be restored if necessary. This is done automatically anyway, but you can also create your own restore points before installing new software – in case this causes problems.

- ❏ Floppy disks must be fully formatted before they can be used.

- ❏ If you want to reuse a disk with old files on it, the Quick Format option is the fastest way to erase files.

- ❏ Floppies should be stored safely away from heat, damp and sources of magnetism.

10 Users and networks

User Accounts 132

Changing user details 134

Networking 136

Network Setup Wizard 138

Sharing access 140

Mapped drives 142

Summary 144

User Accounts

Windows XP makes it easy for several people to share the use of one PC. Each user can have their own set of folders and their own customized Desktop and Start menu.

There are two types of account:

- **Limited** users have access to only their own files and those in the *Shared Documents* folder. They can customise their own desktops, and decide their own passwords and the pictures which identify their account.

- **Administrators** have full access to all aspects of the PC – including other users' areas.

You must have Administrator access to create accounts.

Basic steps

1 Click on the User Accounts link in the Control Panel.

2 Click Create a new account.

3 Enter the user's name and click Next.

4 Set the account type.

5 Click Create Account.

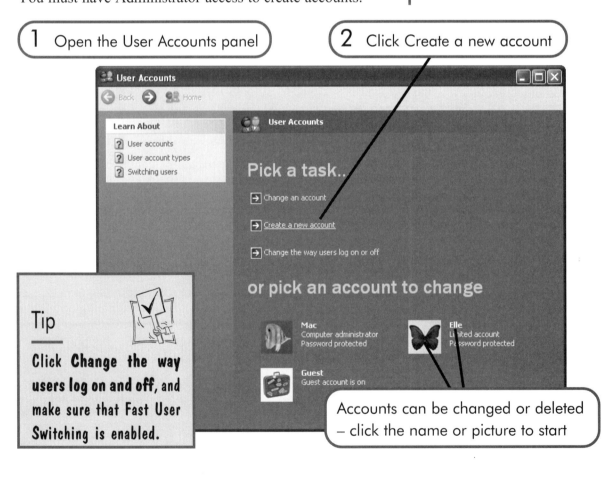

1 Open the User Accounts panel

2 Click Create a new account

Tip

Click **Change the way users log on and off**, and make sure that Fast User Switching is enabled.

Accounts can be changed or deleted – click the name or picture to start

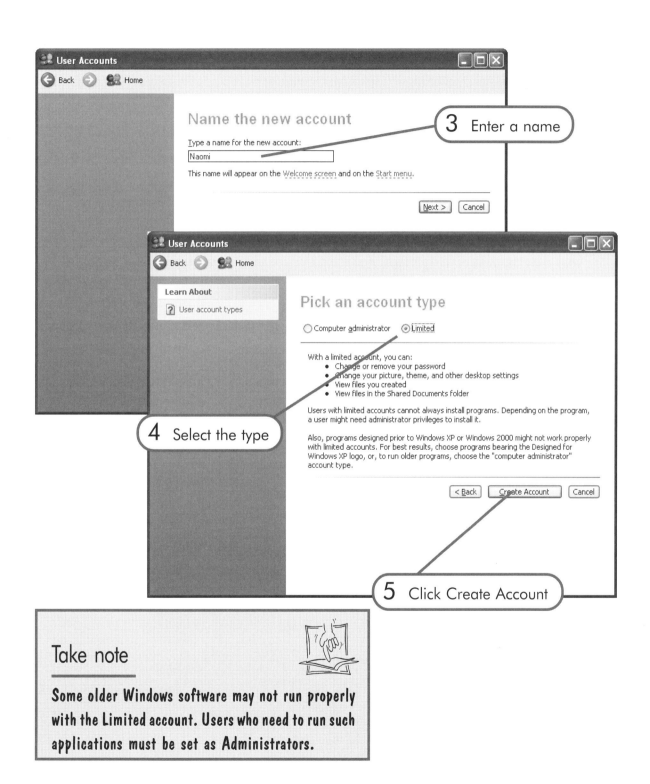

Take note

Some older Windows software may not run properly with the Limited account. Users who need to run such applications must be set as **Administrators**.

Changing user details

Limited users can change only two aspects of their accounts: the password and the picture which appears on the welcome screen and the Start menu. Administrator users can change all aspects of their own – or any other user's – account, including the account type. Changes can be made at any time.

● Passwords can be a pain and should only be created if needed. If you do create a one, click the **Prevent a forgotten password** link in the Related Tasks and create a 'password reset' disk. This will enable you to recover all your data should you later forget the password.

Basic steps

1 Click the User Accounts link in the Control Panel.

❑ Administrators now need to pick the account.

2 Click Change my picture.

3 Select an image from the offered set or click Browse for more pictures to use one of your own files.

4 Click Change Picture.

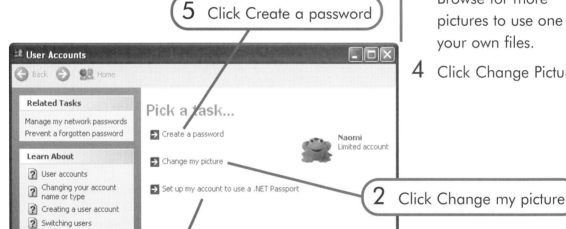

5 Click Create a password

2 Click Change my picture

.NET Passports are accepted at many Internet sites that use secure systems to protect confidential data – set one up from here if you find that you need one

Take note

The password can be anything, but should be something that you can remember but that others are unlikely to guess. And the password hint should not be too obvious – it can be seen by other users.

❑ Passwords

5 Click Create a pass-
word.

6 Enter the password
twice – as you won't
be able to read it, this
is to check that you
have typed it correctly.

7 Enter a hint to help
you remember the
password.

8 Click Create Pass-
word.

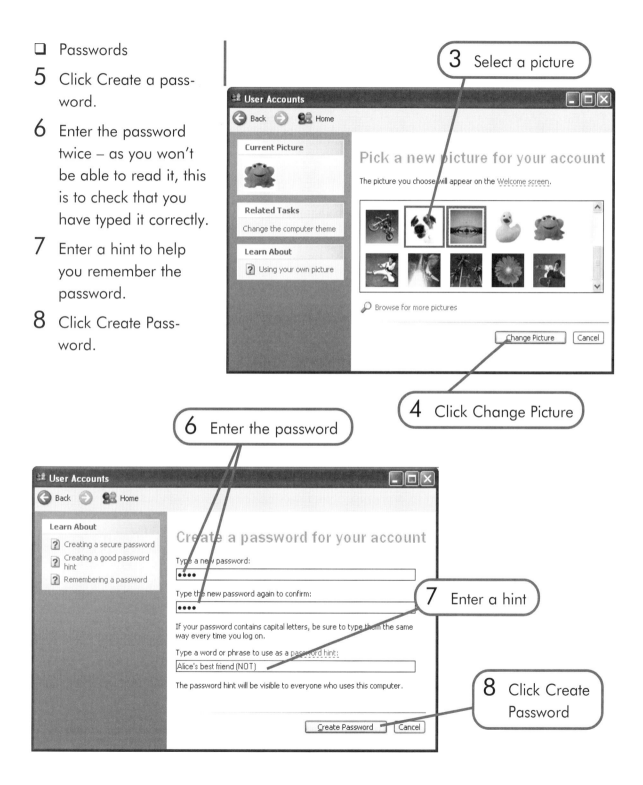

3 Select a picture

4 Click Change Picture

6 Enter the password

7 Enter a hint

8 Click Create Password

Networking

Setting up even a small network used to be a real chore. It got easier with the new tools introduced in Windows 95/98, but it was still not a job for the layman. It's all different with Windows XP. The Network Setup Wizard takes care of setting up the networking software and is easy to use – with two provisos.

- Networking is straightforward as long as you are connecting Windows XP PCs. Connecting to PCs running earlier Windows is possible, but prone to errors and difficulties. If you want to share an Internet connection, the PC with the modem must be an XP PC.

- You still have to open the PCs' cases and fit the network cards, and install their software, then cable them together.

You also need to be familiar with a few basic networking concepts. And in case you aren't, here's all you need to know…

Sharing an Internet connection

If one of the PCs has a modem and Internet connection, and you want people to be able to access this through other PCs, the connection can be shared. As long as the PC with the modem is turned on, the other networked PCs will be able to get online through it without affecting the host PC. If required, the host PC and the others can be all online at the same time through the same connection – though if several people are browsing or downloading at once, things will slow down a little.

Network names

Networked PCs must have names to identify them, which is fairly obvious. Less obvious, the whole set of linked PCs – the 'workgroup' – must also have a name. It really doesn't matter much what you call the workgroup as the name is rarely, if ever, used in a home network.

Network jargon

Workgroup – a set of linked PCs. In a home or small office, all the PCs on the network would belong to the same workgroup. The network in a larger office might be split into several workgroups.

Server – a PC providing a service to the network. A print server shares its printer; a file server acts as a storage place for the data from other PCs.

LAN (Local Area Network) – a set of PCs joined together and sharing files, printers and other facilities.

Ethernet – the most commonly used networking system.

Network hardware

❑ The simplest way to link PCs is with Ethernet cards and cable. You can buy them cheaply, and with the cable fitted with its connectors, from any good computer store. The cards go into an expansion slot – most modern PCs have PCI slots, and at least one will normally be empty.

After fitting the card, you may need to install some software that came with it – read the instructions!

Sharing folders

You can open up some or all of the folders on a PC so that people on linked PCs can read or store files in them. In an office, shared folders would be used for the files that everyone needs to be able to get at – such as the product catalogue, while those holding confidential and/or purely personal files would not be shared.

The Shared Documents folder is initially opened to all network users. Later you can set up sharing for any folder, and allow access at several different levels.

Sharing printers

If a printer is shared, then any networked PC can send files to it for printing. The PC to which it is attached must be turned on, of course, and the person using it may notice that it slows down a fraction as files are shuffled through the printer's folder.

Once the network is set up, use My Network Places to view the other PCs' drives – it works just like My Computer

My Network Places

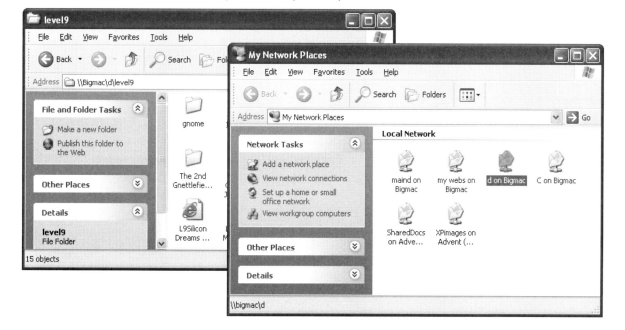

Network Setup Wizard

You can set up your network over time, running the Wizard through each PC whenever you get round to it, but it is probably simpler to do it in one fell swoop. Get all the PCs going, then go round and run the Wizard on each of them in turn.

1 Select the Set up a network option in the New Connection Wizard or *Network Connections* folder.

2 At the Internet Connection stage, tell the Wizard if you want to use the Internet from that PC and whether it is the one with the modem.

3 On the PC with the modem, select the Internet connection.

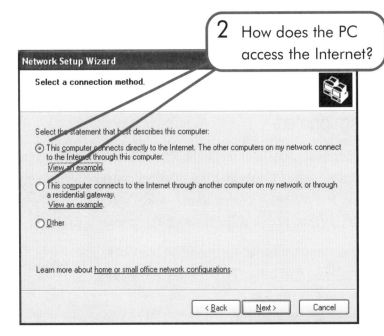

2 How does the PC access the Internet?

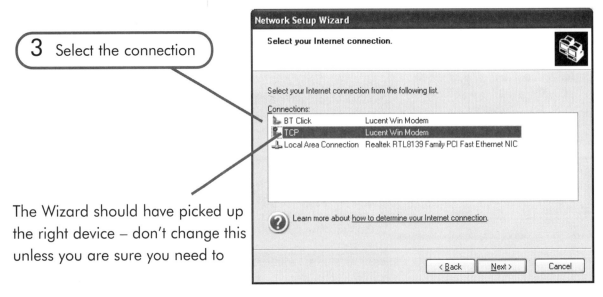

3 Select the connection

The Wizard should have picked up the right device – don't change this unless you are sure you need to

138

4 Enter a name and a description for the computer.

5 Enter a name for the workgroup.

6 Check the summary of the settings, and if everything seems OK, click Next.

7 You will be offered the chance to create a *Network Setup* disk to use on any non-XP PCs that you want to link onto the network.

❑ Restart the PC for the network settings to take effect.

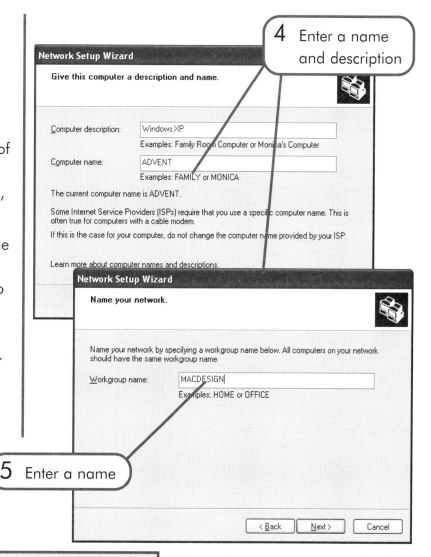

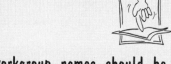

Take note

The computer and workgroup names should be single words, and keeping them simple is always a good idea. In a home or small office, all PCs would normally be in the same workgroup.

The workgroup name must be the same on all the PCs – if in doubt, stick with the default MSHOME

Sharing access

You can change the levels of access that other users can have to the folders and printers on a PC at any time. The changes take effect immediately – you don't have to restart the PC.

- If a folder is shared, others can read and copy its files, but they can only change or delete existing files if you allow them.

- If you share a drive, then all of its folders are shared in the same way.

- Printers are either shared or not, though you can set a password.

❑ Sharing printers

1 Open the Printers and faxes folder from the Start menu.

2 Right-click on the printer and select Sharing...

3 Turn sharing on.

4 Enter a Share name.

5 Click ⬚ OK ⬚.

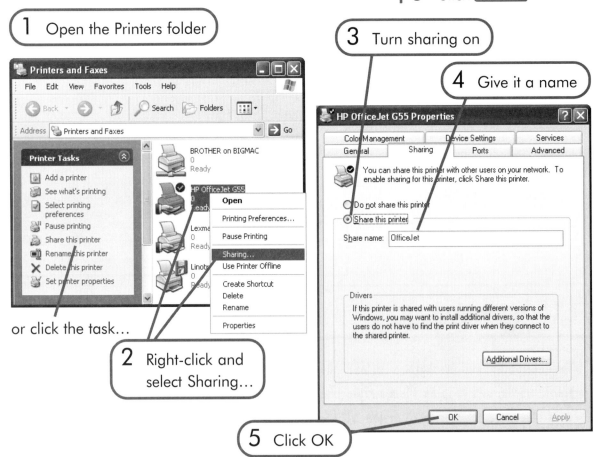

or click the task...

1 Open the Printers folder

2 Right-click and select Sharing...

3 Turn sharing on

4 Give it a name

5 Click OK

Basic steps

❏ Sharing folders

1 Run Windows Explorer or My Computer.

2 Right-click on the folder and select Sharing and Security…

3 Turn sharing on or off as required.

4 Enter a Share name.

5 Turn on the Allow network users to change my files option only if you are sure they will be safe.

6 Click [OK].

If you want to share a folder with others on the PC, but not on the network, drag it into the Shared Documents folder

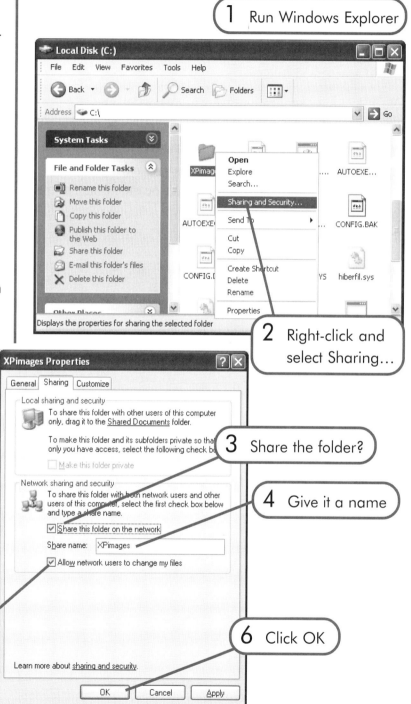

1 Run Windows Explorer

2 Right-click and select Sharing…

3 Share the folder?

4 Give it a name

5 Let others change your files?

6 Click OK

Mapped drives

Most of the newer Windows software can handle network connections with no trouble. When you want to open or save a file, these applications will let you reach across the network and link to any shared folder.

Older Windows applications were often not designed for use on networks, and will only allow you to reach files on drives on the same PC. Fortunately, Windows networking software has a neat solution to this problem. You can *map* networked drives – assign drive letters to them. The C: drive on the PC in the study, for example, which might have a network name of //Study/C/ could then be referred to as F:/ by the PC in the living room.

A drive is mapped once, from Windows Explorer, at the start of a session, and can then be referred to by its assigned letter from within any application.

1 Run Windows Explorer or My Computer.

2 Open the Tools menu and select Map Network Drive...

3 Pick a drive letter – the lowest unused one is probably the best.

4 Type the path or browse to select the drive or folder.

5 If you always need to map this drive, tick Reconnect at logon.

6 Click [Finish].

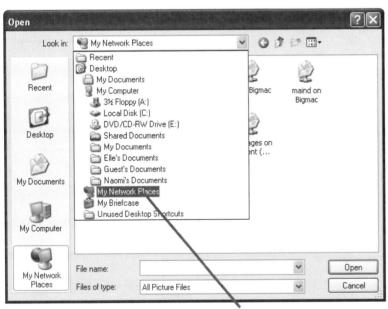

In newer applications, My Network Places is in the Look in list in Save and Open dialog boxes and you can open shared networked drives and folders directly.

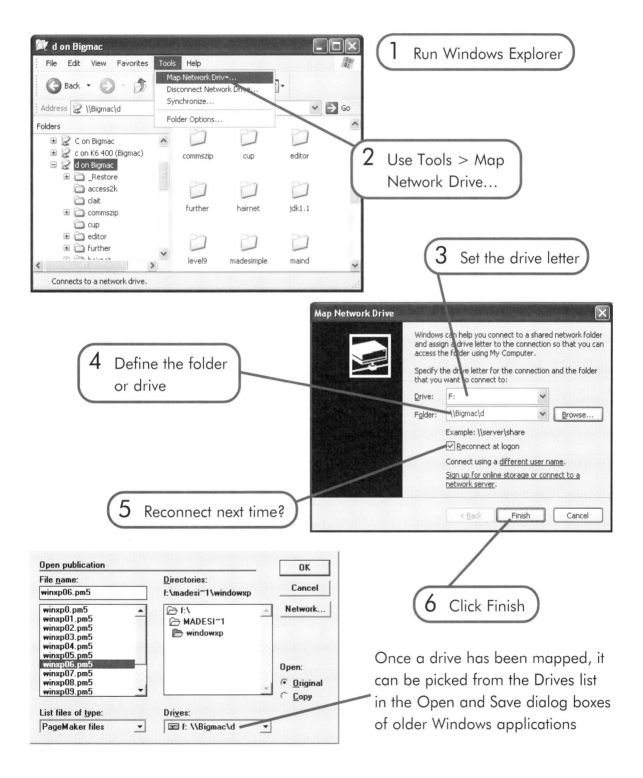

1 Run Windows Explorer

2 Use Tools > Map Network Drive...

3 Set the drive letter

4 Define the folder or drive

5 Reconnect next time?

6 Click Finish

Once a drive has been mapped, it can be picked from the Drives list in the Open and Save dialog boxes of older Windows applications

Summary

❑ If several people use a PC, they should each have a user account, giving them their own safe storage areas and customised Desktop.

❑ Windows XP makes it simple to link PCs into a network so that you can share folders, printers and other facilities.

❑ Once you have get the network cards and cable installed, the Network Setup Wizard will take over and set up the network for you.

❑ You can control the level of access to shared folders and printers, and change the access at any time.

❑ If you have applications which cannot open or save files through the network, you can map network drives to make them behave like a local drive.

11 The Accessories

WordPad 146

NotePad 150

The Character Map 151

Paint 152

The Clipboard 155

Picture and Fax Viewer 156

Scanner/Camera Wizard 158

Media Player 159

Movie Maker 161

Summary 162

WordPad

WordPad is a handy little word-processor, with a decent range of formatting facilities. You can set selected text in any font, size or **colour**, add emphasis with **bold**, *italics* and <u>underline</u>, indent paragraphs or set their alignment, and even insert pictures, clip art, charts and many other types of objects. WordPad has all you need for writing letters, essays, memos, reports and the like. Could you write a book on it? Possibly, as long as it had a simple layout and you were happy to create the contents list and index by hand.

The fact is that most of us, most of the time, use only a fraction of the facilities of Word or similar full-blown word-processors. For most purposes it is more efficient to use WordPad – because it is simpler, it is faster to load and to run – and it's faster to learn!

Tip

WordPad is a good tool for creating and editing the HTML — the coded text that produces Web pages.

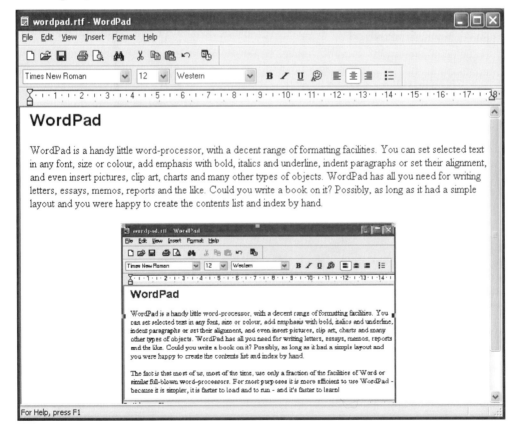

146

Entering text

Tip

One of the great things about Windows applications — especially those from Microsoft — is that they do the same jobs in the same way. Once you have learnt how to enter text, open or save a file, select a font or whatever, in one application, you will know how to do it in the next.

All word-processors have *wordwrap*. Don't press **[Enter]** as you get close to the right margin. WordPad will sense when a word is going to go over the end of a line and wrap it round to the start of the next. The only time you should press [Enter] is at the end of a paragragh or to create a blank line. If you change the margins of the page or the size of the font, WordPad will shuffle the text to fit, wordwrapping as it goes.

Selecting text

A block of text – anything from a single character to the whole document – is selected when it is highlighted. Once selected the text can be formatted, copied, deleted or moved.

When setting alignment or indents, which can only apply to whole paragraphs, it is enough to place the insertion point – the flashing vertical line where you type – into the paragraph.

The simplest way to select text is to drag the mouse pointer over it. Take care if some of the text is below the visible area, as the scrolling can run away with you!

A good alternative is to click the insertion point into place at the start of the block you want to select, then hold down **[Shift]** and use the arrow keys to move the highlight to the end of the block.

Double-click to select a word.

Triple-click to select a paragraph.

Deleting errors

To correct mistakes, press **[Backspace]** to remove the last character you typed, or select the unwanted text and press either **[Backspace]** or **[Delete]**.

Formatting text

You can do formatting in two ways – either select existing text and apply the format to it, or set up the format and then start typing. Either way, the formats are selected in the same way.

Use the **Formatting toolbar** when you want to change one aspect of the formatting – just click on the appropriate button or select from the drop-down lists.

Use the **Font dialog box** when you want to define several aspects, or if you want the rarely-used strikeout effect.

1 Select the text or go to where the new format is to start.

2 Use the Formatting tools.

Or

3 Select Font... from the Format menu.

4 Define the format and click ☐ OK ☐.

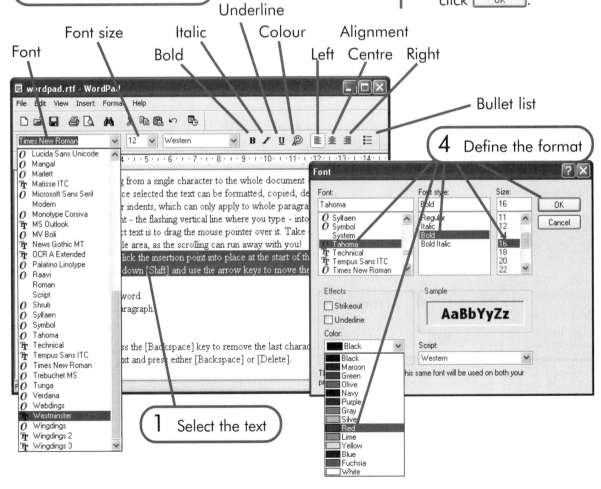

2 Click or pick from a list

Underline

Font size · Italic · Colour · Alignment

Font · Bold · Left Centre Right

Bullet list

4 Define the format

1 Select the text

Basic steps

File > Save and File > Save As

❏ Saving a new file

1 Open the File menu and select Save As...

2 Select the Save In folder.

3 Type in a Name to identify the file clearly.

4 Change the Save as type if necessary.

5 Click [Save].

❏ Resaving a file

6 Open the File menu and select Save.

Or

7 Click 🖫 on the toolbar.

Anything you type into WordPad – or most other applications – is lost when you close the application unless you save the document as a file on a disk.

The first time that you save a file, you have to specify where to put it and what to call it. If you then edit it and want to store it again, you can use a simple **File > Save** to resave it with the same name in the same place, overwriting the old file. If you edit a file and want to keep the old copy and the new one, then you can use **File > Save As** and save the new version under a different name.

In WordPad – again, as in many applications – you can save a file in several ways. The default is Rich Text Format, which can be read by most word-processors and many other applications. You can also save the words, without the formatting, by using one of the text formats.

● If you open a Word document in WordPad, you can save it again in Word format.

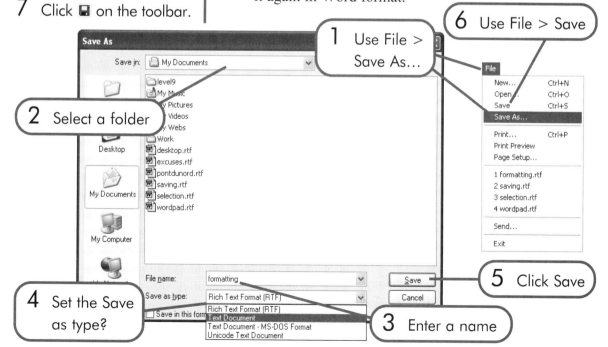

1 Use File > Save As...

6 Use File > Save

2 Select a folder

4 Set the Save as type?

5 Click Save

3 Enter a name

149

NotePad

Notepad is a text editor – not a word-processor – and is an excellent tool if all you want is plain text. It won't do bold or italics or fancy fonts; you can't change the size or colour of the words; it doesn't let you insert clip art or draw diagrams or set text in bullet points. Notepad gives you nothing but plain text files, and that's the beauty of it. Because it is so simple, it is a very small program – 65Kb – which is minute compared to Word (8.5Mb!). Notepad is up and running almost instantly and uses a tiny amount of your system resources.

Use Notepad instead of a word-processor:

● if you have a Hotmail (or other Web-based mail) account and want to compose messages off-line;

● to stash the text copied from Web pages, if you want to edit it before saving it;

● to write the source code for programs in Java, C or other languages;

● or in any other situation where you need unformatted text.

Take note

Notepad can only handle files up to 64Kb - but as that equates to around 9,000 words, it's not too serious a limitation.

The Font... command sets the font used by Notepad for the screen display and printouts. The font is applied to the whole text and is not saved with the file.

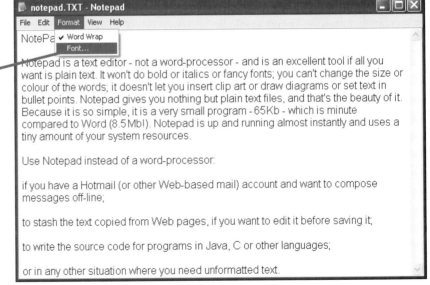

The Character Map

Basic steps

1 Go to the Accessories menu and select Character Map.

2 Select the Font.

3 Click on a character to highlight it.

4 Click [Select] to place it into Characters to Copy.

5 Go back over Steps 3 and 4 as necessary.

6 Click [Copy] to copy to the Clipboard.

7 Return to your application and Paste the characters into it.

This shows the full set of characters that are present in any given font, and allows you to select one or more individual characters for copying into other applications. Its main use is probably for picking up Wingdings for decoration, or the odd foreign letter or mathematical symbols in otherwise straight text.

The characters are rather small, but you can get a better look at a character, by holding the mouse button down while you point at it. This produces an enlarged image.

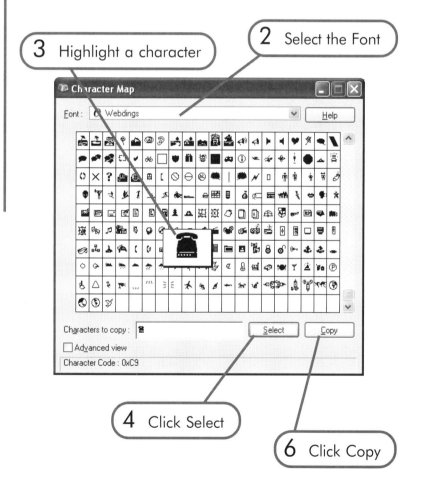

3 Highlight a character

2 Select the Font

4 Click Select

6 Click Copy

Tip

If you click on a character and keep the button held down, you can browse around the map, with each character being enlarged as you move over it.

Paint

There are essentially two ways to draw an image on a computer. In applications like Microsoft Draw (supplied with Works, Word and other Office programs), the picture is made up of lines, circles, text notes, etc., each of which remain separate, and can be moved, deleted, recoloured or resized at any point.

Paint uses the alternative approach. Here the image is produced by applying colour to a background, with each new line overwriting anything that may be beneath. Using this type of graphics software is very like real painting. You can wipe out a mistake while the paint is still wet, but as soon as it has dried it is fixed on the canvas. (Paint allows you to undo the last move; some will let you backtrack further.)

Tip

Press [Prt Sc] to copy the whole screen to the Clipboard, or [Alt] + [Prt Sc] to copy the active window. The image can be pasted into Paint and saved. That's how the screenshots were produced for this book.

Use the Text toolbar to format text – turn it on via the View menu

Ovals are defined by marking the rectangle that they will fit into, making it almost impossible to draw concentric circles. This target was created by drawing the inner circles elsewhere on the screen, then selecting them and dragging them into place.

Basic steps

❑ Option area

The options depend upon the tool:

Free-form/rectangle select and Text – transparent or opaque background;

Eraser and Airbrush – size;

Magnifier – level 2×, 6× or 8×;

Brush – size and shape;

Line and curve – thickness;

Rectangle, Polygon and Oval – outline or fill only, or both.

Tip

Hold down [Shift] when drawing for regular shapes – [Shift] makes ovals into circles; rectangles into squares and only allows lines to be drawn at 0°, 45° and 90°.

The Toolbox

There is a simple but adequate set of tools. A little experimentation will show how they all work. The notes below and on the next page may help.

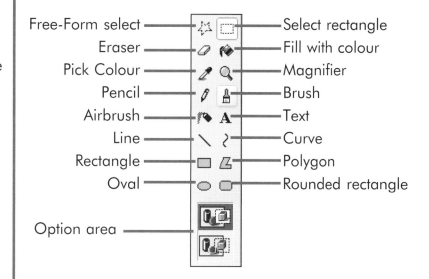

To use the Erase, Pencil, Brush or Airbrush: click to leave a dot or blob; drag to create a line.

To draw a line: click where the line is to start and drag the end into position – you can move the line as long as you keep the button held down.

To draw a rectangle or oval: click at one corner of where the shape is to go and drag to the opposite corner. The shape will be drawn in the current line thickness – switch to the **Line** tool first if you want to change this.

Drawing a curve

The curved line tool is a bit trickier than the rest. Even when you have the hang of how this works, it will still take you several goes to get a line right!

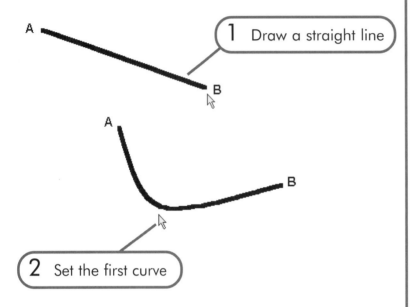

1 Draw a straight line

2 Set the first curve

3 Set the second curve

4 Click at the end

Basic steps

1 Draw a line between the points where the curve will start and end.

2 Click or drag to create the first curve – exaggerate the curve as it will be reduced at the next stage.

3 Drag out the second curve now – as long as the mouse button is down, the line will flex to follow the cursor.

Or

4 For a single curve, just click at the end of the line.

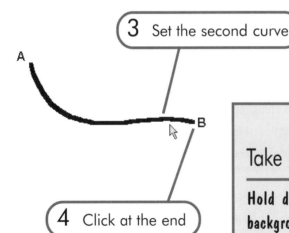

Take note

Hold down the right button to draw lines in the background colour instead of the foreground colour.

Hold it down while using the eraser, to replace any current foreground colour with background colour.

Basic steps

❑ Mixing colours

1 Double-click on a colour in the palette or use Colors > Edit Colors.

2 At the Edit Colors dialog box, click on a Basic or Custom Color and go to Step 6.

Or

3 Click [Define Custom Colors >>] to open the full box.

4 Drag the cross-hair cursor in the main square to set the Red/ Green/Blue balance, and move the arrow up or down the left scale to set the light/ dark level.

5 Click [Add to Custom Colors] if you want to add this to the set.

6 Click [OK] – the new colour will re-place the one currently selected in the palette on the main screen.

Colours

The colour palette is used in almost the same way in all Windows programs. You can select a colour from the palette – use the left button for the foreground colour and the right button for the background –or mix your own. Remember that you are mixing light, not paint.

● red and green make yellow;

● green and blue make cyan;

● blue and red make magenta;

● red, green and blue make white;

● the more you use, the lighter the colour.

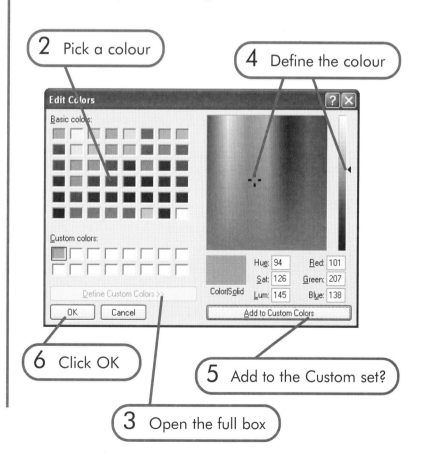

2 Pick a colour

4 Define the colour

6 Click OK

5 Add to the Custom set?

3 Open the full box

Picture and Fax Viewer

This is not actually an 'accessory' – you won't find it on the menu – but it's a very handy utility. You can use the Viewer to copy, delete or print your pictures, and – of course – view them.

Once you have opened the viewer for one file, you can use it to work through all the images in the same folder.

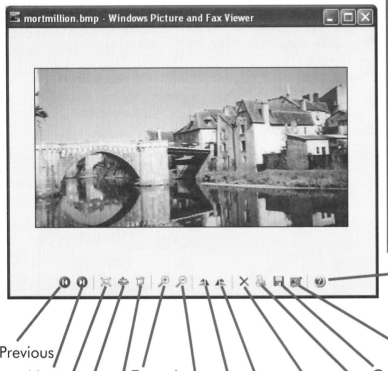

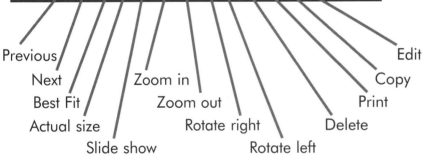

Previous
Next
Best Fit
Actual size
Slide show
Zoom in
Zoom out
Rotate right
Rotate left
Delete
Print
Copy
Edit

Help

Basic steps

1 Open the folder in My Computer.

2 Double-click on an image, or right-click on it and select Open With > Picture and Fax Viewer.

❑ Slide Show

3 Click 🖳 Slide Show to start the show.

4 Click the mouse button or use the arrow keys to move through the images.

5 Press [Escape] to end.

Take note

The Edit command closes the Viewer and opens the image in Paint or other graphics software.

Basic steps

1 Click 🖨 Print to start the wizard.

2 Tick the pictures that you want to print and click [Next >].

3 Scroll through the Available layouts and select one, then click [Next >].

Printing from the Viewer

The print routine takes advantage of the fact that the Viewer works with the whole folder, and not just with a single image. You can select any number of pictures (from the same folder) at a time, and print them individually or several to a page, in a range of sizes.

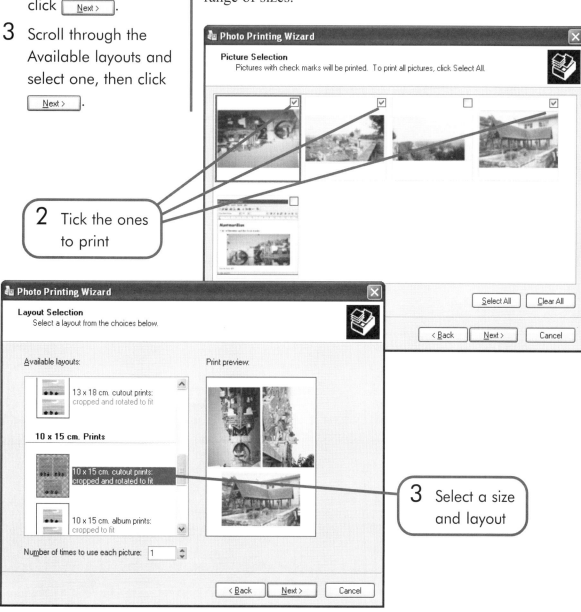

2 Tick the ones to print

3 Select a size and layout

Scanner/Camera Wizard

You can use this to take images in from a scanner or a digital camera, and store them in a folder.

After the picture has been captured, you will be given the option of also publishing the images on your Web site or ordering printed copies from an online photo printers.

❑ Scanning and saving

1 Run the Wizard. It will call up the control panel for the scanner.

2 Click [Preview] and wait while the image is scanned.

3 Adjust the area to be scanned, then click [Next >].

4 Specify the name, format and folder, click [Next >] and wait.

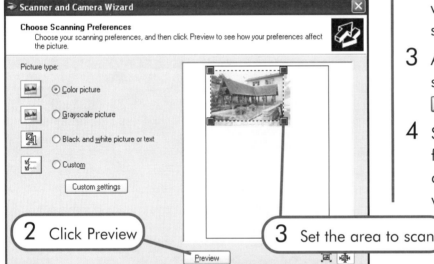

2 Click Preview

3 Set the area to scan

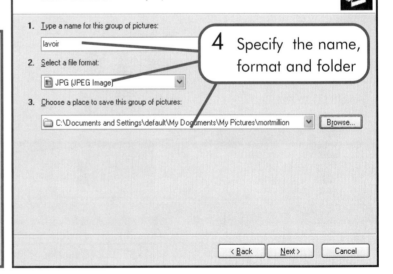

4 Specify the name, format and folder

Tip

If you want to take an image into a graphics program for editing, start from within that program — look on the **File** menu for **From Scanner or Camera** or similar command.

Media Player

Basic steps

❑ Playing CDs

1 Load the CD and wait for Media Player to start up and read in the track data.

2 To change the order of a track, click on it, then drag up or down.

3 To skip over a track, right-click on it, and choose Disable from the shortcut menu.

Media Player is a multi-purpose audio/video player. It can handle sound files in MIDI and in WAVE, the native Windows format, as well as audio CDs and video in the Video for Windows (AVI), Media Audio/Video (WMA and ASF) or the many ActiveMovie formats.

Audio CDs

If you want music while you work, let Media Player play a CD for you. The CD will play the tracks in their playlist sequence – this can be the standard order or edited as required. It's worth taking time over this, as any choices or other information that you enter here are recorded by Windows in a file (stored on the hard disk) and will be reused next time the same CD is loaded.

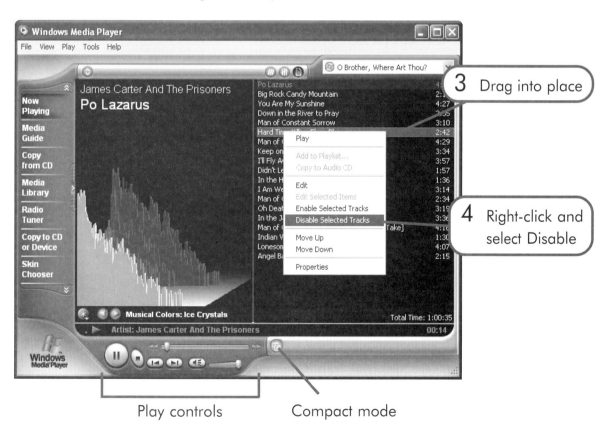

Play controls   Compact mode

Video

New, fast hardware and better software has greatly improved the quality of videos on PC. They are still not that brilliant to look at, but the files are relatively small. 1Mb of video gives around 90 seconds of playing time, and if you are downloading it over the Internet – from a Web site or via e-mail – it will take up to 10 minutes to come in. That's not a bad download to play time ratio. It makes it quite feasible to e-mail home movies to distant relatives – or to put them on your Web page for any friends (or visiting strangers) to download. And there's Movie Maker to do the editing – see opposite.

Skins

Once the video or CD is playing, you can switch into *Compact mode*. This occupies less screen space, and has some great 'skins'. Click **Skin Chooser** and pick one from the list.

When audio is playing, the Media Player screen displays a 'visualization' – a light show that responds to the music. There are dozens of these. To try them, open the View menu, point to Visualization, select a set then pick from one there. Their names are a poor guide as to their nature. You have to watch them to see what they are like.

Tip

CD audio tracks and files, from the Internet or elsewhere, in **MP3, WAV, WMA** or **ASF** formats can be copied through Media Player onto your **MP3** player or other portable device.

Take note

The Radio Tuner is simply another way to get to the Internet Radio facility (see page 174).

In Compact mode, Media Player runs in a skin (above) with a minimal set of play controls. The rest of the commands and controls are reached through the icon (right)

Movie Maker

This can edit digital video, taking images in directly from your camera. The video is automatically split into clips, which can be split further or trimmed and set into a new sequence. You can merge in other clips, or add still pictures, for titles and credits, or a voice-over or background music. It's simple to use, and just the job for editing home video. Trim the half-hour birthday video down to the highlights, add your titles and voice-over and save it as a Movie Maker file. You can then share it with your distant friends and relatives via the Internet in two ways:

- Send it by e-mail. Files are increased in size by 50% when attached to a message (because of the way data travels via mail), but e-mail normally comes in at 3Kb+ per second.

- Upload the file to your home page. Download times from the Web are typically less than 2Kb per second.

Movie Maker is simple to use, but efficient. It's a shame the picture quality isn't quite there yet.

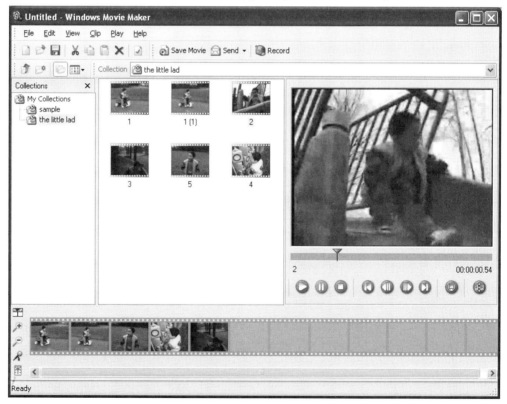

Summary

❏ WordPad is a powerful little word-processor with all the facilities that most of us need most of the time.

❏ Notepad is a text editor – a very efficient tool for handling plain text files.

❏ The Character Map allows you to select special characters from a selected font, to paste into an application.

❏ You can use Paint for creating simple (or complex if you're good enough!) colourful pictures or for editing screenshots and other images.

❏ The Clipboard is used for copying text and graphics within and between programs, and for copying files across disks and folders.

❏ The Picture and Fax Viewer offers a very convenient way to view, print and manage picture files.

❏ If you want to save images to file, the Camera and Scanner Wizard can make life easier.

❏ Media Player will play audio CDs, radio braodcasts or videos. The player can be run in compact mode, in a colourful skin.

❏ With Movie Maker you can edit home videos before sending them to friends via the Internet.

12 Exploring the Internet

Internet Explorer (IE) 164

Starting to explore 166

The History list 167

Favorites 168

Searching in Explorer 170

Windows Update 172

Radio stations 174

Outlook Express 176

Summary 178

Take note

To get online, you must have an account with an Internet Service Provider. If you do not have one already, you will find all you need to connect to AOL in the Online Services folder, and a link to MSN on the Desktop. AOL offers a free month's trial – give it a go.

Internet Explorer

Internet Explorer (IE) is a browser – software for surfing the World Wide Web. IE6 (the current version) is very easy to use.

The main part of the window is used for the display of Web pages. Above this are the control elements. The **Menu bar** contains the full command set, with the most commonly used ones duplicated in the **Standard Toolbar**.

● The **Address** shows you where you are. You can type an URL (Uniform Resource Locator – an Internet address) here to open a page. Typed URLs are stored here, for ease of revisiting.

● The **Links** offer an easy way to connect to selected places. Initially, they connect to pages on Microsoft's site, but you can replace them or add your own.

The **Toolbars** can be turned on or off as needed, but if you want the maximum viewing area open the **View** menu and select **Fullscreen** – (you can add the Fullscreen icon to the toolbar if you find this useful).

The **Explorer Bar** can be opened on the left to give simpler navigation when searching (page 170), or using the Favorites (page 168) or Internet radio (page 174) or History (page 167).

The **Status Bar** shows how much of an incoming file has been loaded. This can also be turned off if you don't want it.

The Standard Toolbar

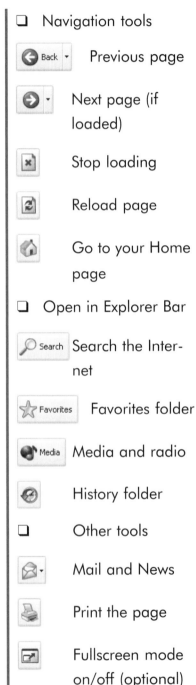

❏ Navigation tools

  Back ▾   Previous page

  ❯ ▾   Next page (if loaded)

  ✖   Stop loading

  ↻   Reload page

  🏠   Go to your Home page

❏ Open in Explorer Bar

  Search   Search the Internet

  Favorites   Favorites folder

  Media   Media and radio

  ⊘   History folder

❏ Other tools

  ✉ ▾   Mail and News

  🖨   Print the page

  ⤢   Fullscreen mode on/off (optional)

Basic steps

❏ Display options

1 Click on View.

2 Point to Toolbars and turn them on (✔) or off from the submenu.

3 Click on Status Bar to turn it on or off.

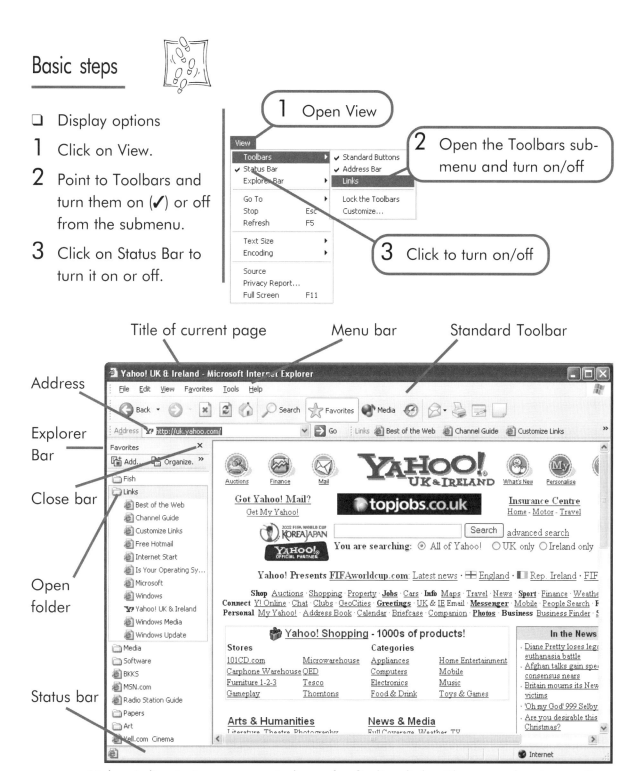

1 Open View

2 Open the Toolbars sub-menu and turn on/off

3 Click to turn on/off

Title of current page

Menu bar

Standard Toolbar

Address

Explorer Bar

Close bar

Open folder

Status bar

Yahoo! directories are great places for finding links. There are local ones for many countries, plus the central one at www.yahoo.com

165

Starting to explore

The World Wide Web is held together by hypertext links. These take you from one page to another – which may be within the same site or on the other side of the world.

Links are easy to recognise – the mouse pointer turns into a hand  when over a link; and even easier to use – just click on them.

But first you need a place to start! IE has some ready-made links to good starting places in the Links toolbar and the Favorites list, and if you know an address, you can type it in directly.

1 Run IE 🗘 from the Desktop, the Quick Launch Toolbar or the Programs menu.

2 Click on a Link.

or

3 Follow a Favorite.

or

4 Type in an Address.

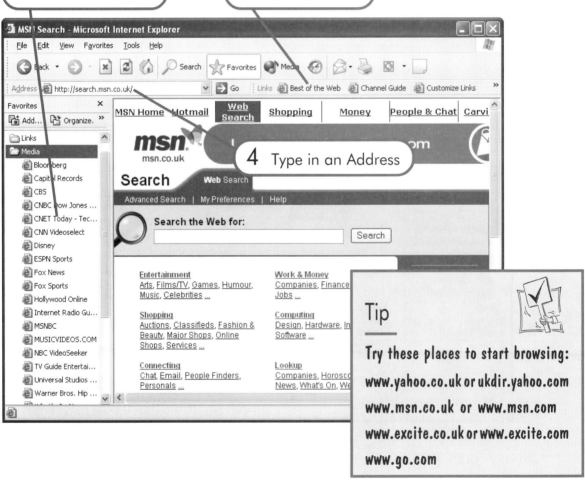

Tip

Try these places to start browsing:

www.yahoo.co.uk or ukdir.yahoo.com

www.msn.co.uk or www.msn.com

www.excite.co.uk or www.excite.com

www.go.com

Basic steps

1 Click the History button to open the list in the Explorer Bar.

2 Click to open a site's folder.

3 Select the page.

4 Click the X at the top right of the Explorer Bar to close it.

The History list

As you browse, each page is recorded in the History list as an Internet Shortcut – i.e. a link to the page. Clicking the History button opens the list in the Explorer Bar, where the links are organised into folders, according to site.

History Offline

If you want to use the History after you have gone offline, open the File menu and turn on the Work Offline. If a page actively draws from its home site – typically to get fresh adverts – you will not be able to open it offline.

Unwanted items can be removed – right-click for the short menu and select Delete

1 Click History

2 Open a site folder

3 Pick a page

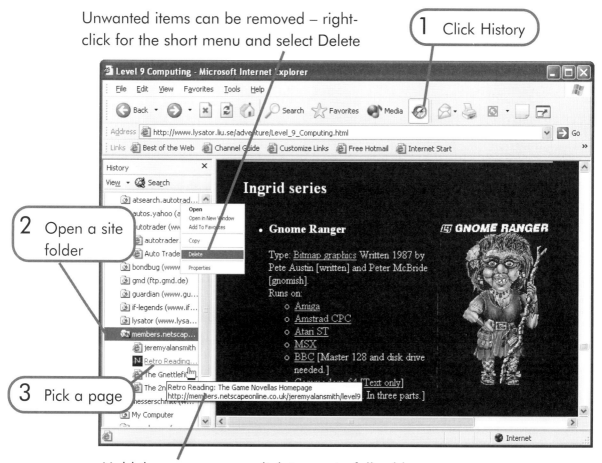

Hold the mouse over a link to see its full address

Favorites

With millions of Web pages available, finding really good ones can take time. When you do find one, you should add it to the Favorites list – this stores the address of the page so that you can get back to it quickly in future. IE has a few Favorites set up for you, to start you off.

You can access Favorites from the Menu bar, but the best way to use them is to open the Favorites list in the Explorer Bar.

● If you want to go back to a page in a later session, you can simply pick it from the Favorites menu.

● You must have the page open to be able to add it to the Favorites – but you can do this offline by opening the page from the History list.

● The Favorites are stored in a folder. If you have a lot of entries, you can organise them into new folders within this, creating submenus of Favorites.

❑ Using Favorites

1 Open Favorites and select the page title.

❑ Adding Favorites

2 Open the Favorites menu and select Add to Favorites…

Or

3 Open Favorites in the Explorer Bar and click 🔖 Add… .

4 Edit the name.

5 To add it to the main menu, click [OK].

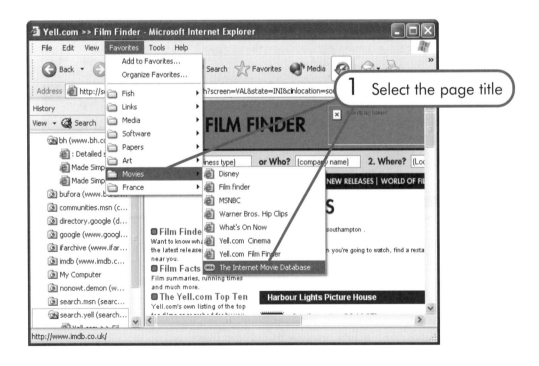

1 Select the page title

Or

6 To store it in a folder, click [Create in >>].

7 Select the folder.

8 Click [OK].

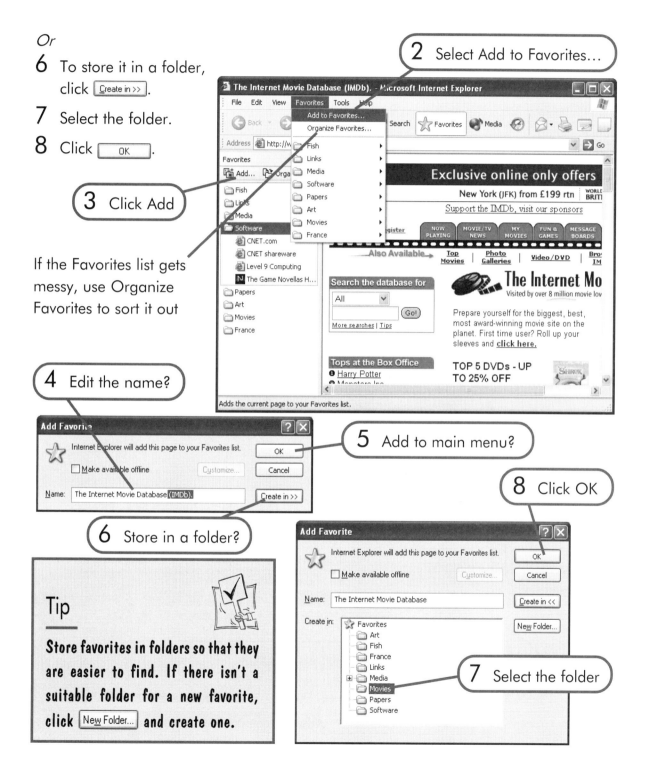

2 Select Add to Favorites...

3 Click Add

If the Favorites list gets messy, use Organize Favorites to sort it out

4 Edit the name?

5 Add to main menu?

8 Click OK

6 Store in a folder?

7 Select the folder

Tip

Store favorites in folders so that they are easier to find. If there isn't a suitable folder for a new favorite, click [New Folder...] and create one.

Searching in Explorer

Directories like MSN and Yahoo are good for dipping in to see what's around, but if you want specific information on a topic, you are probably better off with a search. You can run a simple search in the Explorer Bar for Web pages, maps and other things. This uses the Excite 'search engine', one of the best of many such on the Web.

The Explorer Bar is a convenient way to handle searches as you can switch easily between viewing results and running new searches, but it may not always work that well. If it doesn't find any good links – in fact, it is more likely to find too many than too few – then try working directly at a search engine, where you will be able to define your search more closely. Two of the best search sites are **www.google.com** and **www.altavista.com**.

Basic steps

1 Click the Search tool.

2 Select the Category.

3 Enter a keyword or phrase.

4 Click [Search].

5 You are taken to Excite for the results – click a link to view the page.

6 If you don't find what you want, try a new word or widen the search to the whole Web.

It doesn't matter where you are when you start the search

1 Click Search

2 Select a category

3 Enter the keyword(s)

4 Click Search

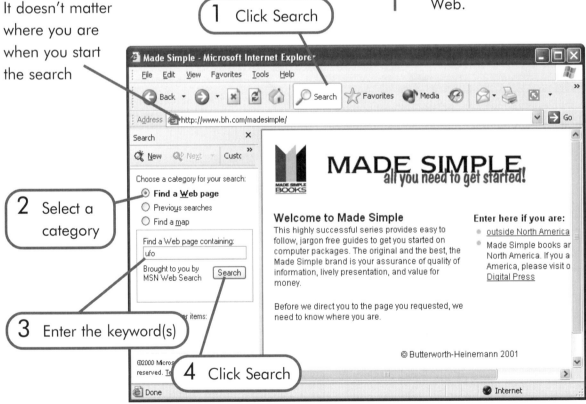

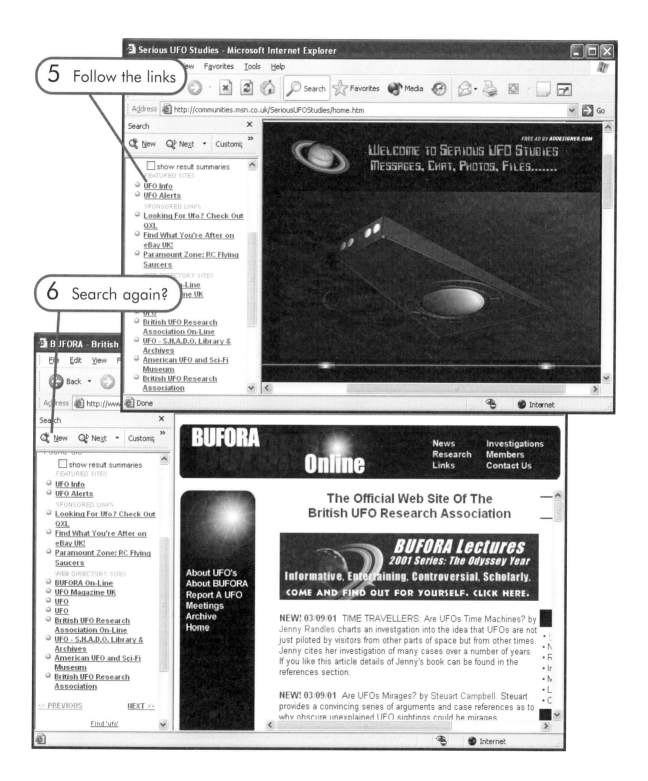

Windows Update

Microsoft regularly produce improvements and bug-fixes for Windows, distributing them through the Internet. Windows has an Automatic Updates routine which can connect regularly to Microsoft's site to get the latest patches and additions.

The Automatic Updates settings can be changed through the **System Properties** item in the Control Panel. It can:

● download automatically, notifying you when the files are ready to be installed;

● alert you if it finds any new critical or optional updates;

● be turned off completely, if you prefer to use the Windows Update link to check the site when it suits you.

1 Run IE.

2 Click the Windows Update link, or select it from the Links folder of the Favorites.

3 Wait while the Update Wizard scans your PC.

4 Scroll through, selecting the updates that you want.

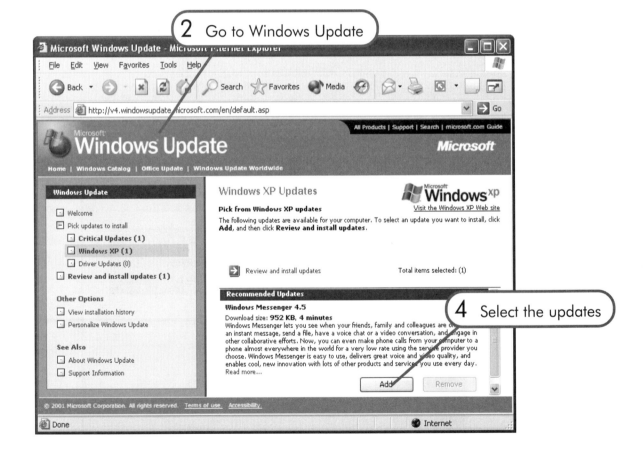

5 Check the selection and click Install Now.

6 Wait while the software is downloaded and installed.

The time estimates are fairly accurate – make sure that you have enough time to get the files before you start, as some can take quite a while to download

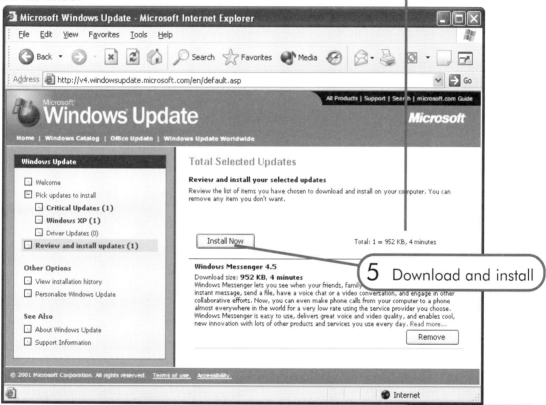

5 Download and install

6 Watch and wait

The files are downloaded and then installed automatically. You will normally have to restart the PC to bring them into play, but it doesn't have to be done immediately – finish your session as usual. At the next start up, there will probably be a delay while your system files are updated.

Radio stations

Over the last few years, new techniques have been developed for transmitting audio (and video) over the Internet in real time. Now you can listen to a 'broadcast' through Internet Explorer, and you can browse the Web or pick up your e-mail at the same time.The sound quality is as good as you would get from a portable radio, though if you are also trying to download other stuff you will get occasional breaks in transmission.

The key question, of course, is why not just use your radio? If you can get the station on the radio, it makes little sense to use your browser, but can you pick up American Family Radio, KBAY of San José, Dallas Police Scanner or OzRock? You can through the Web.

When you link to a radio station, a small window will open for the broadcast, and usually another for the station's site – you do not have to keep it open to listen. The broadcast will not start immediately as there is always an initial delay while the first block of data loads in. Internet Radio is not quite in real time. Incoming data is stashed in a buffer – temporary storage – and played from there, to try to smooth out irregularities in the flow of data.

Basic steps

1 Click the Media button to open Media in the Explorer Bar.

2 Select Radio Guide. This links to Windows Media which has links to radio stations all over the world.

3 Click the My Stations ⬦ icon if you want to listen to a station from your own selection.

4 Click ⏬ by a station to display its details then click Play.

Or

5 Click Find More Stations to explore and choose from their huge selection.

6 If you find a good station, add it to you My Stations set.

7 Drag the slider ▬▬▮▬ to set the volume.

8 When you have done or if you need to speed up other downloading, click ▣.

Tip

You'll find another good selection of stations at http://netradio.com

174

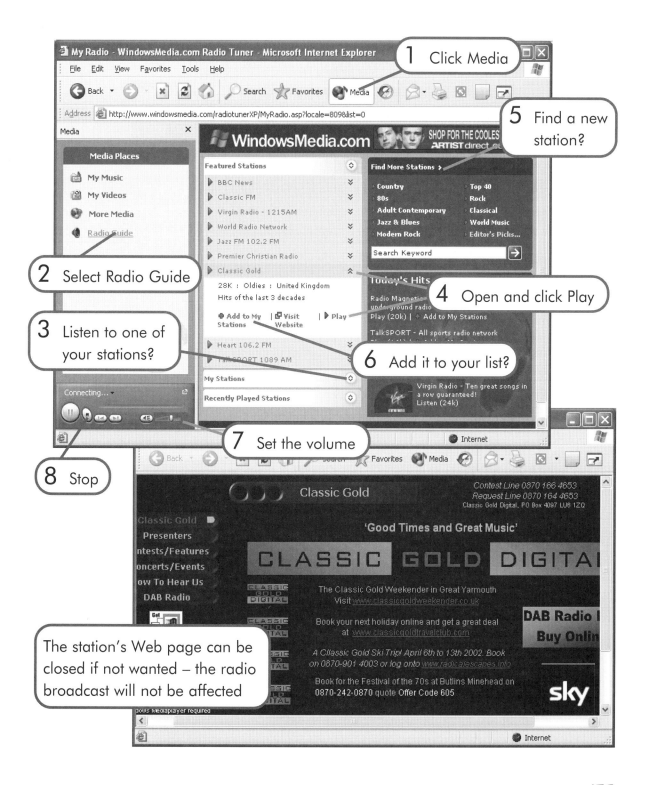

1 Click Media

5 Find a new station?

2 Select Radio Guide

4 Open and click Play

3 Listen to one of your stations?

6 Add it to your list?

7 Set the volume

8 Stop

The station's Web page can be closed if not wanted – the radio broadcast will not be affected

Outlook Express

The World Wide Web may be the most visible and entertaining aspect of the Internet, but it is not the only one. The other two major aspects are e-mail – which for many people is its most valuable use – and the newsgroups (where enthusiasts exchange ideas on specific topics).

Outlook Express will handle your e-mail and newsgroup access efficiently. Messages can be composed and read offline, so that you only need to connect briefly once or twice a day to send and receive new ones – keeping phone bills to a minimum.

Take note

There are over 50,000 newsgroups, covering just about every topic under the sun! Check them out – there's sure to be at least one for your job, hobby and obsession.

The headers of messages are shown here. They tell you who sent the article, when, and what it's about. Select one to read it in the lower pane.

Use these tools to reply to or forward on the current message

1 Click New Mail

2 Pick your stationery

Folders for mail and newsgroups are listed here

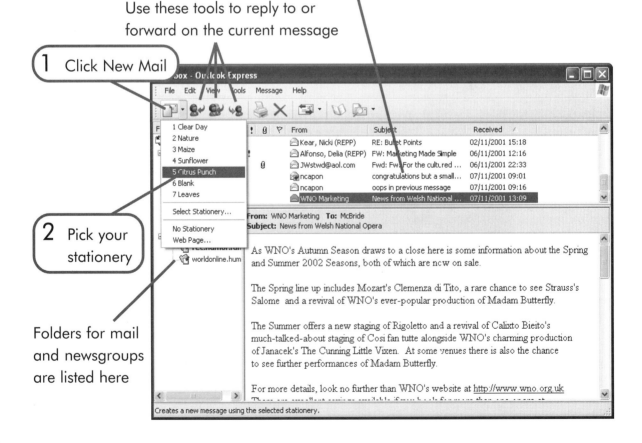

Sending a message

Or

2 Select your stationery
   from the New Mail list.

3 Type the address or
   click 📖 To: to pick from
   the Address Book.

4 Type a Subject so that
   your recipients know
   what it's about.

5 Type your message.

6 If you want to attach a
   file (that video?) click
   📎 and select the file.

7 Click 📧. The mes-
   sage will either be sent
   immediately or go into
   the Outbox to be sent
   when you are next
   online and click 📧 ▾.

To send a message all you need is the address – and something to say. Actually, if you are replying to a message, you don't even need the address as Outlook will pick that off the incoming mail. Addresses can be typed in or picked out of the Address Book – click **Addresses** in the main toolbar to open it.

Messages can be composed and sent immediately if you are online, or composed offline and sent later.

Messages are normally written as plain text, but if you are writing to someone who can read HTML-formatted messages (such as another Outlook user) you can liven them up by using stationery – with backgrounds and fancy fonts.

A message can be sent to several people at once. You can put them all in the **To:** box, or send some as copies in the **Cc:** box.

Take note

Stationery can add a lot to
the transfer time.

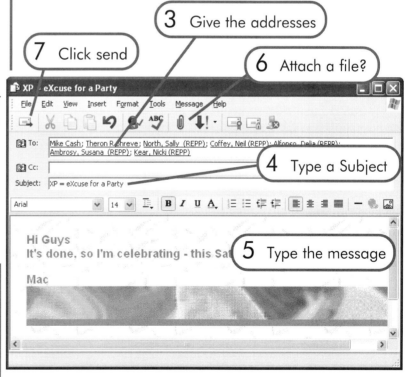

3 Give the addresses

7 Click send

6 Attach a file?

4 Type a Subject

5 Type the message

Summary

❑ Internet Explorer is a Web browser. It is integrated into My Computer and Windows Explorer, so you can also start to browse from there.

❑ Browsing is simple – just follow the links – but you need a place to start. IE comes supplied with links to some good start points on the Web.

❑ The History list gives you an easy way to revisit sites – online or offline.

❑ The Favorites folder stores links to selected places on the Internet. There are some already set up and you can add your own links.

❑ You can search for stuff in the Explorer Bar, then view the resulting pages in the main screen.

❑ Go online to the Windows Update site from time to time to see if Microsoft has any new or improved versions of its Windows XP software.

❑ Many radio stations broadcast through the Web. You can listen to them in IE using the Media option in the Explorer Bar.

❑ Outlook Express is the supplied software for handling e-mail and newsgroup articles.

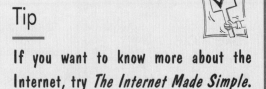

Tip

If you want to know more about the Internet, try *The Internet Made Simple.*

Index

A

Accessibility 102
All Programs menu 10
Administrators 132
Allocation units 118
Application extensions 52
Applications Help 16
Arranging files in Explorer 62
Arranging windows 34
Audio CDs 159

B

Background 94
Backup 120
Bad sectors 118
Branch 43
Browser 164
Browsing 45
Buttons, radio 7

C

Cascade 34
Category View 90
Character map 151
Check boxes 7
Child 43
Classic View, Control Panel 90
Click 4
Clipboard 155
Clock, setting 87
Closing windows 39
Colour schemes, Desktop 95
Colours, Paint 154

Compatibility modes
    for older Windows applications 73
Contents, Explorer 46
Contents, Help 17
Control menu 30, 33
Control Panel 90
Copy 155
Copying files 66
Crashes 13
Cross-linked files 118
Cut and Paste 67, 155

D

Date and Time, adjusting 87
Deleting files 68
Deleting folders 59
Desktop 2
    customizing 94
Desktop Cleanup Wizard 76
Details view 48
Dialog boxes 6, 26
Disk > Format command 128
Disk access speed 119
Disk Cleanup 123
Disk Defragmenter 119
Display Modes, changing 33
Display options, My Computer 48
Documents 9
Double-Click Speed, mouse 97
Drag and drop 4
Drivers 52, 110
Drop-down lists 7

E

E-mail 176
Edit > Invert Selection 65
Edit menu 155
Error-checking 118
Ethernet 136
Explorer 42
Explorer display 46
Explorer, split between panes 63
Extension, to filename 44

F

Fast User Switching 132
Favorites 168
File > Save 149
Files
    copying 66
    deleting 68
    finding 70
    moving 66
    names 44
    selecting 64
    types 77
Filmstrip view 48
Floppy disks 128, 129
Folder List 47
Folder Options 52
Folder structure 43
Folders 43
    creating 56
    deleting 59
    expanding 54
    moving 58
    sharing 137
Fonts 104

Formatting a floppy 128
Formatting text 148
Fragmented disks 119

G

Graphical User Interface (GUI) 2

H

Hard disks 43
Help
    applications 16
    contents 17
    find 20
    on icons 27
    search 19
High Contrast displays 102
History 167
Hypertext links 166

I

Icons, for files 48
Icons view 48
Index, Help 18
Installing fonts 104
Internet Explorer 164
Internet Shortcut 167

K

Keyboard 5
    Accessibility 102
Keyword 19

L

LAN 136
Languages, adding keyboards 101
Limited users 132
Lists, Drop-down 7

Log on/off 11
Lost fragments 118

M

Mapped drives 142
Maximize 30, 33
Media 174
Media Player 159
Menus, selecting from 6
Minimize 30, 33
Mouse 4
  adjusting 97
  keyboard equivalent 103
  pointers 97
Movie Maker 161
Moving files 66
Moving the Taskbar 81
Moving windows 36
My Computer 42, 47
My Network Places 42

N

Network Drives, mapping 142
Network hardware 137
Network Setup Wizard 136
Newsgroups 176
NotePad 150

O

Outlook Express 176

P

Paint 152
Parent 43
Passwords 135
Paste 155

Paths 44
Picture and Fax Viewer 156
Pointers 97
  customising 98
  resize 37
  shape 31
Print queue 112
Printers
  adding 110
  settings 108
  sharing 137
Printing, cancelling 112
Printing from file 113
Printing photos 157
Programs, running 10
Properties 8, 72
Properties, of folders 55

Q

Query icon 26

R

Radio buttons 7
Radio stations 174
Recycle Bin 68, 69, 123
Regional Settings 100
Registered file types 77
Restart 12
Restore 30, 33
Restoring files and folders 69, 122
Root 43

S

Saving files 149
Scanner and Camera Wizard 158
Screen Savers 96

Scroll bars 31, 38

Search engine 170

Searching the Web 170

Selecting files 64

Selecting text 147

Server 136

Sharing access 140

Sharing folders 137

Shortcuts 74

Show Desktop 32

Shut down 12

Size of window 37

Skins 160

Slider 31, 38

Sounds 99

Start menu 9

   adding to 85

   customising 84

Status line, Explorer 46

Sub-folders 54

System files 52

System Restore 124

System tools 116

T

Tabs 7

Taskbar 33, 80, 81

   Toolbars 82

Text, formatting 148

Themes 92

Thumbnails view 48

Tile 34, 35

Tiles view 48

Title bar 30

Toggle switches 6

Toolbar, Customizing 51

Toolbar icons, Explorer & My Computer 47

Toolbox, Paint 153

Troubleshooters 23

Turn Off 12

U

Uniform Resource Locator 164

User Accounts 132

User details, changing 134

V

Video 160, 161

View options, Explorer 62

W

Wildcards 70

Windows 30

   arranging 34

   changing the size 37

   closing 39

   modes 32

   moving 36

Windows XP Help 22

Windows Update 172

WinZip 21

WordPad 146

Wordwrap 147

Workgroup 136

Y

Yahoo! 165